RANDOM SHOTS - MICROBLOG SHARPENERS FOR YOUR NETIZEN SKILLS

RANDOM SHOTS - MICROBLOG SHARPENERS FOR YOUR NETIZEN SKILLS

A WHETTING STONE TO SHARPEN YOUR PROFESSIONAL WRITING

DR. R. DIVAKAR, PHD

PARTRIDGE

To order additional copies of this book, contact
Partridge India
000 800 10062 62
orders.india@partridgepublishing.com

www.partridgepublishing.com/india

Preface

Why this book?

In this netizenship era, energized focus comes with sharp and arsenal like words and sentences for your blogs and postings.

For professionals a compact repository of crisp usages can be handy and immensely helpful for expression of fertile thoughts. Your thoughts should not remain poor cousins to your limited word and sentence power.

The book precisely helps you as ready reckoner for the sharpest usage for the context you are in..

It contains thousands of good words and sentences collected over a period of 3 decades by a seasoned development professional. The collection of sharp words and sentences is coterminous with the advent of netizenship.

This is the era where the good old concept of "we write - you read" from the so called traditional writers has been disappearing fast. Now it is mutuality of communication where you are also as powerful writer as someone you read about.

So this book helps unearth a potential writer in you out of your in built fertile thought processes and takes you to higher orbits of professional writing and blogging skills.

How to use this book as ready reckoner

Just randomly open book and keep on through the lines for a matching word or sentence in sync with your ongoing thought process about what you wanted to express bridging gulf between mind and finger.

That's it; you will be elevated to the next stage professional writing competency.

This book goes stronger and stronger if you enrich it with your own good finds

I have worked hard to compile so many words and usages over 3 decades for you and I have all faith that you will find a profound link in this book as you graduate to a accomplished writer.

That's how my friends have named it aptly as "Random Shots".

Praise for the Random Shots

I wanted to write an appropriate sentence for my book. Divakar's compilation and random collection of good words and sentences and the huge compilation helped me to pitch in good sentences wherever needed instantly. You can also try and just brisk through the pages till you stumble upon the good piece you had in mind as thought.

Dr. Ranjit Voola,
Associate Professor
Sydney University Business School
Author of "Markets and Strategy", an Asia Pacific Edition

I am a development professional and preparing professional presentations is part of my daily life. Whenever I am struggling to get a good word or sentence I go through the pages of "Random Shots" and adapt the core idea and contextualize to my presentation. It really helps you unearth your latent but fertile thought processes

Dr. Christopher Fredrick
Senior consultant
Asia Pacific Region, Bangkok
World Vision International
Author of several books on Development Strategies related to poverty

It's beautiful thing when career and a passion come together. Divakar's book "Random Shots" is precisely useful when your thoughts are derailing for want of right words and here is the book that helps keep it back on track

Dr. Kallu Rao
Associate Professor
College of Commerce
Omen
UAE

Fluid boundaries

Predatory markets

Life leaps like a geyser for those who drill through the
rock of inertia
    - Alexis Carrel

Macro fundamentals

Finite disappointment is defeated by infinite hope

Micro management

Syncretic approach

Segmenting the market

Generic proclivity

A prayer for the day:

–Father, thou knowest I am growing older. Keep me from becoming talkative and possessed with the idea that I must express myself on every subject.

–Release me from the craving to straighten out everyone else's affairs.

–Keep my mind free from the recital of endless detail. Give me the wings to get to the point.

Energized focus

Meat on the bone

Consolidating the top; fragmenting the bottom

Swelling bottom

Imposing new externalities

It is poor cousins to other programs

Matrixed management

Alternate variant

Spirited horse

Targeting the determinants of gaps than out comes

Rule of thumb training

Let go off things not meant for you

Key quality life indicators demonstrate value to social investors

---

Inner child in both of them simply wants to connect and love the other

---

To a man with hammer every problem looks like a nail

Need to get off their high horse

Governing a large country is like frying a small fish. You spoil it with too much poking.
 — Lao-tze

Law must respond to society's cry for justice

Negative people have problem for every solution; Positive people have solution for every problem

---

Addictive solitude

In admiring tone

Profound link

Its excellent rendition

Unproductive stress

Mitchell's Law of Committees:
Any simple problem can be made insoluble if enough meetings are held to discuss it.

He unspools his charm

Intellectual depth

Managerial bench strength

China aspires to India's advantage as Anglophone country

Milking more out of innovation than manufacturing
Eg., I phone manufacturer gets 20US$ out of 600 $ for manufacturing

---

Caterwauling about flight of jobs in the country

It scavenged detritus of Detroit

The question is whether or not you choose to disturb the world around you, or if you choose to let it go on as if you had never arrived
   - Ann Patchett

The President is penciled to visit the place

Just another addition to the country's grave yard of start ups

---

It is this place's ferigueur uniform

Trying to haul themselves up by the boot straps

The country's industrial gear heads

Hobnob with billionaires

In a country where failure on borrowed capital is tantamount to dishonor.....

Pride and principle is hewed into every enterprise

In a world of diminishing mystery, the unknown persists

For every Face Book and Google there are hundreds of ideas that die face down and end in zilch

---

Central to its lore is not stigmatizing honest failure

Agreeability of failure

Being a philosopher, I have a problem for every solution.
— Robert Zend

To fire up tech crucibles

World is now awash with venture money

Only those who risk going too far can possibly find out how far one can go

---

Euphoniously dubbed

Confection of technology and capital

- Seal my lips when I am inclined to tell of my aches and pains, for they are increasing with

the years and my love to speak of them grows sweeter as time goes by.
- Teach me the glorious lesson that occasionally I may be wrong
- Make me thoughtful but not nosey, helpful but not bossy.
- With all my vast store of wisdom and experience it does seem a pity not to use it all, but
- Thou knowest, Lord, that I want a few friends in the end.

Bridging the trust gap

Hell is in the details

Pigeon holing the poor as prudent is naïve

Stress intolerance

Strategic levers to meet the goals

Financial inclusion vs. poverty reduction

Today's greatest labor saving device is tomorrow

Paper work is the embalming fluid of bureaucracy, maintaining an appearance of life where none exists.
— Robert J. Meltzer

Philanthropic capital

Light travels faster than sound, that's why some people appear bright till they open their mouth

---

With blood in his teeth

90% of politics is deciding whom to blame

Liquid table assets

They just make best of everything they have

Happiest people do not have the best of everything

Commercial like rates would price ultra poor out of markets

Remember that there is nothing stable in human affairs; therefore avoid undue elation in prosperity or undue depression in adversity.
    — Socrates

They spend greater part of their life getting their living

Folding into future and not extrapolating to past

Be at peace with yourself always

Champions do not become champions at the ring
They are merely recognized in the ring

Misery index

Skill of communication is hearing what is not being said

We ourselves feel that what we are doing is just a drop
in the ocean. But the ocean would be less because of
that missing drop.
    — Mother Teresa

If we draw HDI for our ultra poor they are amongst
poorest 25 nations in the world; matching low end sub
Saharan Nations

For peace of mind… resign as General Manager of
the universe

Time Plan
    ✓ Capture ideas, wants and needs
    ✓ Commit to block time and resolve your musts
    ✓ Schedule specific time to work on your results
    ✓ Compute measure and celebrate results

To add growth lead followers
To multiply lead leaders

Activity is not necessarily accomplishment

Using excessive share of energy on contentious issues

Anyone can steer the ship but it takes the leader to chart the course

---

Dealing with people is like digging gold;
For 1 ounce gold you have to dig 1 tone soil
But while digging look at gold and not dirt

Self sabotaging thinking process

Chism's Law of Completion:
The amount of time required to complete a programming project is precisely equal to the length of time already spent on it.

There is no objective world - it is set of lenses through which we view the world

---

Life is 10 gear cycle with many gears unutilized

Trifles make perfection and perfection is no trifle

Reserve of negative energy

You cannot play with the animal in you without becoming wholly animal, play with falsehood without forfeiting your right to truth, play with cruelty without losing your sensitivity of mind. He who wants to keep his garden tidy doesn't reserve a plot for weeds.
— Dag Hammarskjöld, *Markings*

Strengthening the weak by weakening the strong

Failure is detour and not dead end

Smooth sea never made a skillful mariner

Lose inhibitions give exhibitions

For me trees have always been the most penetrating preachers
In their highest boughs the world rustles
Their roots rest in infinity
But they do not lose themselves there
- Hermann Hesse

Born to win but conditioned to lose

If you think education is expensive try ignorance

Walking encyclopedia but living failure

I learned long ago never to wrestle with pig
You get dirty; besides the pig likes it

I pay more for the ability to deal with people than for
any other ability under the Sun
    – Rock Feller

Good luck is opportunity meeting preparation

World never cares for our self respect
    – Bill Gates

Life is never justified; you have to get to used to it

Global powerhouse

India should have been rich nation with some poor people

But is poor nation with some rich people

If you find yourself in a hole the first thing to do is stop digging

---

Mind those people who set their watches by your clock

We are nation of religious giants and ethical infants

India is growing in the nights because Government works in the day time

---

If honesty is there nothing else matters and if honesty is not there nothing else matters

---

You have to mesh your thinking

For some of the large indignities of life, the best remedy is direct action. For the small indignities, the best remedy is a Charlie Chaplin movie.

The hard part is, knowing the difference.
    — Carol Tavris, *Anger: The Misunderstood Emotion*

Perpetuality of the institution and philosophy that feels it

A few catalytic interventions will bring in load of difference

---

Co existence of bountiful nature with abject poverty

Compelling synergies

Factory style recruitment

Loading the punch

Hanson's Treatment of Time:

There are never enough hours in a day, but always too many days before Saturday.

Making a case for the most marginalized

Learning journey

Matrix with thematic Managers

Pay band

Your mission interests us and we can effectively contribute

Thanks a bunch for your instant reply

Its Google territory

Have close eye to the bottom line

New service delivery architecture

Sending you hugs from our family

Most people get married believing a myth — that marriage is a beautiful box full of all the things they have longed for: companionship, sexual fulfillment, intimacy, friendship. The truth is that marriage, at the start, is an empty box. You must put something in before you can take anything out. There is no love in marriage; love is in people, and people put it into marriage. There is no romance in marriage; people have to infuse it into their marriages.

A couple must learn the art and form the habit of giving, loving, serving, praising — keeping the box full. If you take out more than you put in, the box will empty.
  — J. Allan Petersen, Homemade

Eco system of the society de-bars poor from occupying equitable position in value chain

---

Shaky moral compass

The radical power of humility

When nothing goes right, go left

There is a place in my life that you alone can fill

Authority without wisdom is like a heavy axe without an edge: fitter to bruise than to polish
— Anne Bradstreet

All I want is someone who will stay no matter how hard it is to be with me

---

There is free cheese in the mouse trap and it is called subsidy for the poor

---

Don't dig up in doubt what you have planted in faith

--

Try to be rainbow in someone's cloud

The singer stretched the melodic horizon further

Of the broken bow, two persons are in fear
   - Afghan Proverb

Overarching contribution

You carry his heart and courage

Lone ranger

Strand of thought

In order to defray part of secretarial expenses

Collective vs. Profit maximization firm

Withered many storms

Skewed decisions

Breaking the bread by opponent

Outside of traffic, there is nothing that has held this country back as much as committees

---

Age gracefully? I think not. Age ferociously instead. Seize everything valuable within reach. Extend.

Question. Give. The face will follow. All the cosmetic surgeons in the world could never produce such a face.
— Roger Rosenblatt

Give up things that weigh you down

It is leaning against the wrong wall

If you want to keep camels, make your door high
- Arabian saying

The first step towards wisdom, is to be aware that there are other points of view as worthy as yours

---

Gap between profits and compassion

Exploring the middle ground

Philosophers only interpret the world; the point is to change it

---

Very specific market segment that has not been reached very successfully so far by the sector i.e. the poorest of the poor (people living below $1.25 per day income threshold)

If you can meet with triumph and disaster and treat both the imposters same
    – Wimbledon court wall writing

Enlarging the vortex of Indian investment economy

Vulgar display of inefficiency

Hope quotient

When you lose do not lose the lesson

None are as empty as those who are full of themselves
    – Benjamin Whichcote

Silence may be misinterpreted but never misquoted

Beware – items in the calendar are closer than you think

The manner of living is more important than the standard of living

---

High interest rates attract only desperate borrowers

Success doesn't mean the absence of failures; it means the attainment of ultimate objectives.

It means winning the war, not every battle

Repository of commercially scalable technologies

Mispricing

It is sublime manufacturing industry

Eco mark of products

"There are two ways to pass a hurdle: leaping over or plowing through... There needs to be a monster truck like option."
   - Jeph Jacques

Those who understand us, enslave something in us

Unbelief is something stems from strong belief in another

The Program is not a linear step but a spiral and cyclical process.

The process should move forward to new program cycle

Assorted livelihoods resources

Blending traditional wisdom with frontier technologies

Gender is social construct and sex is biological construct

It evidences solid ground management abilities

For discerning polls

Contradictory genetic richness but food hungry

Bio diversity led poverty reduction

Pro nature, pro poor and pro women programs

It took time to find its strong roots

Water has gone deeper
You just need a longer rope

Every cloud has silver lining

Degradation of forests beyond ecological revival

Anyone can hold helm when the sea is calm

Fat cats

Gerrold's Laws of Infernal Dynamics:
1. An object in motion will always be headed in the wrong direction.
2. An object at rest will always be in the wrong place.
3. The energy required to change either one of these states will always be more than you wish to expend, but never so much as to make the task totally impossible.

De human conditions

Perpetual holiday is good definition of hell

In every war they kill you in a new way

Landscape of the dispossessed

Extremely practical and hands on approach

When two men in business always agree, one of them is unnecessary
   - <u>William Wrigley Jr.</u>

It has notably minimal foot print in Asia

Cause driven and profit driven

Building a contingent response strategy for the program

Emerging experiences

B etter ware out than rust out

In the world of international trade, the .... sector looked like rock star

---

Inspiring collection of success stories, piling up breathless superlatives and arm waving proclamations

---

Extreme poor live so close to the edge that they have to scramble more than the rest of us to avoid go hungry

---

Smoothening consumption

A man does not have to be an angel in order to be saint

Flocking to it in droves

Share holders value maximization

Biting the bullet

Split identity

Driving the transition

Stifling air of buttoned formality

Frog in boiling water and frog in warm water

Diametric opposite

Transitional hiccups

No good deed goes unpunished.
   - <u>Clare Booth Luce</u>

Lone wolf playing the social card

Big banner project of Organization

Social value to customers; economic value to investors

Migration cycle and academic cycle

Egregious reason

Vulgar achievements

How safety nets can be coordinated with micro finance to create pathways for the poorest out of extreme poverty

---

Truncated life history (abridged) approach

Ethnographic research

Secondary key informants

Thought leadership

Profit pragmatism

Save social objective for which it is founded

The award of recognition makes us feel more grounded to say there is huge responsibility

---

It serves to complement rather than condemn itself

It looks like the team has lot to be proud of

Force character

Smart is when you believe only half of what you hear
Brilliant is when you know which half to believe.
— Robert Orben

Micro owning should precede micro lending

To shape our thinking on key development topics

Inspired detective work

Downward transition back to poverty

Gender division of labor

Specific market segment that has not been reached by formal sectors effectively

---

Deliverables seem too aggressive

Tragic flaw

Communists read Marx and Non Communists understand it

Unlocking people's potentiality

He is like a grass mover in the cemetery, lots of people under him but nobody pays attention to him

---

The maximum effective range of an excuse is zero

Multi layered filters within poverty - there is extreme poverty line

---

Ultra poverty is the most pervasive threat

Poverty premium

Meets at half way

You are the average of the five people you spend the most time with
    - Jim Rohm

Unbalanced and misleading portrayal

Sweeping generalization based on anecdotal information

Climbing steadily out of poverty

It has raised the quality bar within the product range

It makes farfetched leaps of logic

Stult's Report:

Our problems are mostly behind us. What we have to do now is fight the solutions

---

It contains accumulated evil of the whole political system

Big lies are delivered with the precision of a metronome: thanks to an omnipresent, repetitive media and its virulent censorship by omission

---

The secular iconography is embedded in our consciousness

It stained the consciousness of the world

Human beings are the only creatures that allow their children to come back home
   - <u>Bill Cosby</u>

National fetishism

Hollywood can reverse the history

Defeatism

This is the age of forensic satellite evidence

If we remain silent victory over us is assured and a holocaust beckons

---

I grew up in cinematic diet of religious glory

The sovereign is he who decides exception

You are with us
Otherwise against us…. approach

I believe in American exceptionalism with every fiber of my being
    - Obama

Petro dollar is a pillar of American global power

It is a shattering read

Soft underbelly of growth

Multivariate indices factored to measure sustainable
Graduation from poverty

Poverty conscious and prosperity conscious

Decentralized collegial body

Civil society needs both head and heart
Bleeding heart alone will not work

The joy of being imperfect

Harmonized with ongoing program

Market led solutions

I could just bounce off them

The subject technically does not fall under mandated
purview of organization

Our foundation typically invests in social development

Don't throw away the old bucket until you know
whether the new one holds water
— Swedish proverb

The program design intersects with your orientation to look at critical issues as we are graduating them to access better amenities

---

Feeding the mind with canned chatter

Lowering the threshold level of poverty – it is ultra poverty

---

Double inclusive

When I got enough confidence, the stage was gone.

When I was sure of losing, I won.

When I needed people the most, they left me.

When I learnt to dry my tears, I found a shoulder to cry on..

When I mastered the skill of hating, Someone started loving me from the core of the heart..

And While waiting for light for hours when I fell asleep, the sun came out..

That's LIFE!! ---

No matter what you plan, you never know what life has planned for you

---

Success introduces you to the world.

But Failure introduces the world to you...

Often when we lose hope and think this is the end, God smiles from above and says, "Relax, sweetheart; it's just a bend, not the end!!

If I have any merit, it is getting along with individuals, according to their ways and characteristics....At times it involves suppressing yourself. It is painful but necessary.... To be a leader you have got to lead human beings with affection.
  - JRD – TATA

Humans have built a mindset of permanency out of an apparently temporary life...sort of building castles out of bubbles and wanting more bubbles to build more castles

---

Promoting pro-poor research on innovative community-based approaches and technological options to enhance field-level impact

---

Adversity is another way to measure the greatness of individuals.

I never had a crisis that didn't make me stronger
  - Lou Holtz

Nonperforming ratio

Interest pricing curve and Income curve

Building inclusive financial sectors

Intrinsic eminence

Power shared is power multiplied

Let us not break our own fences

Hanging onto bitterness and resentment is like eating poison and expecting somebody else to die
— Unknown

Half concerns

Nobody has sunk in his own sweat

"To the people of poor nations, we pledge to work alongside you to make your farms flourish and let clean waters flow; to nourish starved bodies and feed hungry minds. And to those nations like ours that enjoy relative plenty, we say we can no longer afford indifference to suffering outside our borders."
- President Obama

To eschew violence

It makes eminent sense

Fragile liberal space

Pick up points in every stop

Capacity ranking of Groups

Turf war

Lineal descendant

Episodic events

Evolved structure Vs Loaded structure

Forward area

What you do, speaks so loud that I cannot hear what you say.
   - Ralph Waldo Emerson

Over liquid poor

Thoughtful summary

Prisonal environment

Defying DNA

Photo shopped pixels

Your soul and spirit transcend the body

Your face is not what you are

Antiquated methods

Consumed by his own self image

Opinionated

Moving with hares hunting with hounds

Deadly rationalization

Reports are now written in four tenses: past tense, present tense, future tense, and pretense, defined by the imperfect past, the insufficient present, and the absolutely perfect future

---

Invisible chains

Distance between ideal and real is directly proportional to hypocrisy

---

Unhappiness is equal to the trade between what you want most and what you want at the moment

---

Integrating the ultra poor into economic circuit

Throwing the gauntlet

The thin veneer of cohesiveness protects them from bitterness of life struggles

---

At the end of the day we must create wealth and not distribute poverty

---

Negative self talk

Inclusive financial sectors

Bundling and monetizing loans

Painfully undercapitalized sector

Social deserts

Needs should be reduced to kind of possessions

Digital divide

Zero tolerance recovery

Wading through thick mass of bureaucracy

Dead rope

Supplier driven fallacy

Miniscule outstanding

Shift from donor fund to debt finance

Spatially overextended operations

Experience is tempered by social sector background of individuals rather needs of enterprise to exercise financial discipline

---

Putting faith in abilities

Hold baton and not drumstick

Weiner's Law of Libraries:

There are no answers, only cross references.

Practices are reduced to the level of possessions

Lack of bargaining power is equated with market potentiality

Spreading the resources over several activities

Collective unconscious

Moving from fringe to mainstream

Happiness is not achieved by the conscious pursuit of happiness;

It is generally the by-product of other activities.
   - <u>Aldus Huxley</u>

Collateral advantage

Fruit of great cultivation

Chip of choice

Some financial institutions feed on lack of bargaining power and helplessness and call it market demand

---

Society and system satisfy everybody's need but not greed
   - MK Gandhi

Uncultivated food

Homogenized society

Self divinization

Finagle's Laws of Information:
   1. The information you have is not what you want.
   2. The information you want is not what you need.

3. The information you need is not what you can obtain.
4. The information you can obtain costs more than you want to pay

---

Verbal magic patterns on the looms of rhetoric

A regressive condemnation without providing space for improvisation

---

The issue is going to be not solved tomorrow nor have we entirely surmounted the cyclical darkening of relations but they are breathing easier

---

With heartening, burgeoning of people to people relations

Tin pot

Soldiers march on their stomachs

I am so glad I had a childhood before technology took over

Genius is fruit of relentless hard work

Failed genius is a proverb

Smacks of archaic mental fixation and reaction

People say walking on water is miracle but to me walking peacefully on earth is the real miracle
  – Thich Nhat Hanh

Apply and supply syndrome

It is not encrypt on stone but is a process

Replicable protocol

Borrowers attitude and bankers aptitude are mismatching

Pie in the sky

Where growth is exponential

Months and years instead of capabilities and motivation decide how long it takes for you to make it to the next role

---

Grow at a pace that challenges your intellect and motivation

Feeling constrained and underutilized

Coveted credentials

Employee orientation and domain depth

Leveraging the best of all worlds

Community intimacy

Solid conceptual and analytical frame work

Specific elements of marketing cycle

If you can find something everyone agrees on, it's wrong.
   - <u>Mo Udall</u>

You are never given a dream without also being given the power to make it true
   - Richard Bach

Green consumerism

Adding muscle to their finances and resources

Travesty of justice

Confluence of ideas, convergence of efforts and common vision

---

Shaping the outcomes

Your mission interests me and I can effectively contribute

Spend and keep money in mind and not in heart

Multiple bottom line businesses

Mutual distrust

Lessening foot prints

Primary small producer is the lowest entity in the supply chain

---

Skewed scale of success

Yearlong cash flows

Entrepreneurs are example and not the exception

De risking operational zones

Universal constants

Toxic popularity

People's bio diversity register

Sunrise sector

To chart new developmental paths

From tickling to bubbling

Never produce what you can't sell and never attempt to sell that you can buy cheaper

---

Vision of better lives and we still hold fast that vision

Poverty line can't be monetized alone

Idea incubator

All that is necessary for the triumph of evil is that good men do nothing

---

Do not pray for easy lives; pray to be strong men

Do not pray for tasks equal to your power but power equal to your tasks

---

Burdening ourselves with opinions

Geography is destiny

Find fortune in failure

You can't chose your neighbors

---

10 lessons of Life
1. Take charge - leadership is within and not outside
2. Earn your happiness - we know the value if it is hard earned
3. Nothing succeeds like failure
4. When you lose do not lose the lesson
5. Excellence is not destination it is journey
6. Respond and not react response evaluates with calm mind reactions make us to the way what other want us to do
7. Be physically active never succumb to time pressure and sacrifice your health
8. Never compromise on your core values one must define what you stand for
9. Play to win It brings out desire to stretch out
10. Give back to society

Currying favors

Trepidations

Muzzling the dissent

Incremental approach

Geo ethnic milieu

Think globally act locally

The greatest good you can do to others is not sharing your riches but to reveal to them their own
    - Disraeli

Individualized enterprise but collective market

We judge ourselves by what we feel capable of doing while others judge us by what we have already done

---

Amicable disposition

Reverse discrimination

It is lamentable that to be good patriot one must become the enemy of the rest of mankind

---

Press of hot button

Overarching vision

World can be grasped by only action and not contemplation - Hand is cutting edge of mind

---

Let us relate it to bigger picture

Exponential growth

Plagued by

Saddled with procedures

Quality gate

Wheels within wheels

I am caught up with deep sense of let down

No one can make you inferior without your consent

In great attempts it is glorious even to fail

It is more from carelessness about truth than from intentional lying that there is so much false hood in the world

---

Of Holistic production management system that avoids synthetic fertilizers and pesticides minimizes pollution of air, soil and water and optimizes health and productivity of independent communities of life, plants, animals and people

---

From sea line to snow line

Coffee is successful but Coffee Board has failed

Eternal pregnancy

Powering nap

Deconstruction

Good teaching is 10% subject and 90% theater

Negative cycle

'Hand holding' to 'hand in hand' to 'shaking hand'

Creative tension

Job content and job enrichment

Fear is dark room where negatives thoughts are developed

Psychological comfort

Hit a six off the bouncer

Team is not a way but is the only way

Doomed or bloomed

Audacity is equal opportunity trait

Every person you meet is your mirror

God sells all things at the price of labor

Rugged individuality

If everyone is moving forward together success takes care itself

---

Virtue is insufficient temptation

Unflinching look

Negative incentives

Catastrophic illness

Output based model

Supply and demand side issues

Eat a humble pie

Making tacit knowledge public

Virtue and wisdom are two wheels of a life cart

Practice showcasing

Recalcitrant

James bond of the sector

Obligate yourself

Training is everything; peach was bitter almond and cauliflower is nothing but cabbage with college education
– Mark twain

Searching wood for trees

Functional constituents

Concomitant duplication of efforts and resultant conflicts

Key differentiator

Validating statistical premises

Ground truthing

Livelihoods is the means and opportunities for living governed by resource ownerships, skills, access, productivity, entitlements and vulnerabilities at the individual, family and collective levels

---

We are fragrance and government is wind, wind is always vague. But nobody can match its outreach and force but without fragrance it is dry wind

---

Assiduously marketed by left

Catch all phrases

Prisoners of procedures

Let us park our faiths and beliefs in the privacy of our personal lives

---

Accidental geniuses are really hardworking creative souls

Genius is all about human enterprise, the spirit, of scientific enquiry and perseverance

Genius itself is not accident

The harder we work the luckier we get

Emotional foundation

Apples were an innocent fruit

Until they were used to seduce males

Instead of yielding fruit for wine

The grape wine turned to telling tales
    - Al Shuddup Yaar by Bachchoo

Let us adapt to each other's limitations

It is victim of its own anti-thesis

Fragrance has to make friendship with wind

It led us astray

World's greatest under achiever

Past efforts using subsidized and directed credit have left a distressing legacy of failed programmes and created many skeptics

---

Reciprocal lending

Economically active but poor

Reengage mainstream financial sector

Latent demand into effective demand

Building local stake

In deep slumber

Eulogize

Towering presence

Uncertain times when much seems to be crumbling down around us and amongst ruble we see the remains of so many heroes, so many broken shards of impeccable reputations

---

Probity

Bastions of journalistic excellence

Enduring symbol of excellence

Passionate patronage of investigative journalism

Unfazed

Factoring in mass appeal

It found its crusading champion in this sector

No holds barred

To fuel the crusade

Fading into penniless oblivion

Unabashed enthusiasm with which he grasped the slimmest of chances that life offered him

---

Working his way through

Choice
- Conceptual choice

- Strategic choice
- Institutional choice
- Structural choice

Edifying up line leader

Pocket borough

Coming by wind fall

Dead certainty

Hand shaking call

Growth pole

Equality is etiquette

Making deep channels in human life

Micro finance starts at disadvantage for the poor

Their mind is hardwired to know savings

They constitute the lowest denominators

Hatred is powerful motivator

Split hair over disputes

Speaks with measured finality

Beguiling

Doctrinal differences

Drinking from same cup

Fortuitous (accidental)

Vacuous (empty headed)

Springing to mind

Out of witches brew sprang up fenie of ….

The stoutest heart breaks at the roll call of the brightest, this land can offer

---

Box office material

Pseudo liberals chained to altar of ambiguity and expediency

Vacated the ideological high grounds

When you sow the dragon's teeth don't be surprised at what you get

---

Fleet floater

Sink or swim

Disarray

Keeping our hands over delinquency waters

Plummets from....

Potential derivers of loss

You can't look good by making others bad

There is overwhelming reason to quit

Of the total tapestry of the budget to pick out one single thread as being discolored could be unfair to entire structure of budget

---

Putting matter in perspective

Their minds are hardwired for savings

Let us make social pillar under global economy

Market dysfunction analysis

Facilitate flow of commercial capital into micro finance by minimizing the information asymmetry and experiential gap between formal financial sector and micro finance practitioners

---

Notching up twin horses of finance and enterprise

The most potent weapon in the hands of the oppressor is the mind of the oppressed

---

Federation: enumerated powers with the center and residual powers with the constituents

---

Facilitating paradigm shift in sustainable livelihoods diversification and attendant problems like stress migration

---

Elements of Livelihoods
- Adequacy
- Security
- Well being

- Capability
- Sustainability

Livelihoods is pattern of interdependencies between the needs, interests, values of particular individuals, lifestyles and factors shaping it

Livelihoods is adequate stocks and flows of good and cash to meet basic needs

It is security to secure ownership of resources including assets and reserves and to offset risks, ease setbacks and meet contingencies and control over income earning activities sustainable to the maintenance or enhancement of resource productivity on a long term basis

---

5 capitals
- Natural
- Social
- Human
- Economic
- Physical

Congruent (matching)

Insular policies

Elucidation (clarification)

Livelihoods is central to the idea of inter individual net works and organizing practices

Livelihoods is Individuals and groups striving to make living

---

Livelihoods is their attempt to meet
- consumption and economic necessities
- cope with uncertainties
- respond to new opportunities

To chose between different value positions

Conventional anchorage

Community chain

Normative and cultural dimensions of Livelihoods

Sure footed

Compulsive hostility

De Notre

In calcuble

Reverberate

Farthest reaches

Clusters of fiefdoms

Sphere of influence

Hold sway over lives

Throw weight

Adulation

Straight jacket approach

Flood tide

Jostle for position

Steady hand

Party pantheon

The mountains are high and the emperor is far away

Cool headed

Personable

Prickly demeanor

Quintessential

Poised for steady double digit expansion

Getting heard

Unconsolidated debt

The sum of mishappening in their lives is constant

Kind of balancing justice frees ourselves from the rules and obligations one implies on oneself

---

Courage to leap into a new career

To learn the ropes

Radically changing the game

Linear 3 step sequence

It is easier to change organization top down or bottom up but not from middle

---

Live wire

Dark mutterings

Thinking out of box

Enlarging the herd

Leading to the grand path

Latched up

Soft and hard options

Very hard work doubles market value

Fleet floater

Amoeba takes shape as per its own convenience

Pulling their own shoe straps

Only little fingers can't make hand

We have enough religion to fight each other and not enough to love each other
   - Jonathan Swift

Career jam

Peaks and valleys of business cycle

Inflating the intelligence reports

Self goal

Anal itch

Appearing in press for all wrong reasons

Joint sin

Chip in

Lateral thinking

Vertical enterprise - lateral enterprise

Steady the boat

Impulsive instinct for micro enterprise

---

3 D reasons

My brokenness is better bridge for people than my pretend wholeness ever was

---

Serendipity

Lumpanization of India

Every time rise the bar and stretch
Challenge to excellence is within and not outside

To mimic

Juggernaut

Main frame savings to family server Income Generating Programs

---

Cost arbitrage

Each cycle of Income Generating Activity takes family into a different trajectory

---

Launching pad

Growth engine

Logical choice

Tough rural micro and macro environment

Flummoxed (confused) the entrepreneurship

Poor of all hues are terrific entrepreneurs
Their forays are limited in size and ambition due to socio-economically eliminated entrepreneurship

---

Income Generating Programs should give wings to spirit of enterprise

Comparison is starker

Each income generating program cycle should be a sling shot to enhance their trajectory

---

Smirk

Twin engagement of savings and income generating programs

Moral borrow meter

You can't pull down the performer for the sake of parity in fact we should pull up the non performer

---

I have fashioned my life into the sector successfully

Congruent

Lone fern

Paranoia

Burgeoning sector

Espoused objectives

Glacial pace

Fiat accompli

Enjoying both the worlds

Historical obligation

Edifying upline leader

Nobody stands taller than those willing to stand corrected

Bullet proof faith

Vision is seeing future finished in advance

Wheezing old horses

Historical baggage of bad image

Suboptimal solutions

Anathema (abomination - disgrace)

Ease of entry barriers

Pathways out of poverty

Local poverty line

Demand and supply stream; enabling stream

Contextual models

Silver bullet and magic bullet

Be magic bamboo; bend but never break

We go through the life bumping into obstacles we could easily by pass

---

Lashing blind rages at fancied wrongs and imaginary foes

Stellar performance

Not skillful but incredibly soulful

His work is so connected to his heart

At each other's throat

Prisoners' of opinions

Hating is an art

Happily incompatible

Unduly high set up costs

Regulatory inefficiency

Seamless consistent services

Briefing pack

When first line in admin is very strong second line becomes head strong

---

Accepting life uncertainties can paradoxically overcome fear and enhance survival

---

We can draw strength by choosing to celebrate the ordinary pleasures of life even in the shadow of death

---

Negative incentives

Catastrophic illness

Output based model

Supply and demand side issues

Takers eat well givers sleep well

Procrastination and vagueness are fragile spirits

Improbabilities are finger prints of God

Do not pave way but prepare a road map

Steroids of development

There is no perpetuity in civil society arrangements

We have baits and not baskets of fish

Optimal ignorance

New layer of flavor

Never draw comfort from ignorance

Never negotiate out of fear or include fear to negotiate

Two way traffic problems for the poor with savings and credit

But mid course plunge into development sector

Obstacles can't crush me; every obstacle yields to stern resolve

---

He who is fixed to a star does not change his mind

Institutionalization of conflict

Value failure but system success

Firing the gun on other's shoulders

Sure fire

Keeping the heath burning

System driven and process driven

Global resources push against poverty

First generation starts, second grows; third blows

First generation learns, second generation earns, third generation burns

---

Loyalty curve

Change equation in equality

Thought elastic

Transparent evidence based

Notable foot print in inclusive poverty segment

It was an idea refused to die, failures notwithstanding

Cast iron guarantee

Increase in negotiation position

Diminution (decrease)

Success is getting what you want and happiness, wanting what you get

---

Bleeding edge

Silent cog

Rising exponentially

Other side of bottom

Cosmetic qualifications

Ensconced

Headed to slippery slope

More cooking and less offer of menu

Feeling of invulnerability

Unlocking value

Poachers turned game keepers

We can point out and avoid the many pit falls that can catch those who may be less familiar with them

---

Coast on reputation

Attrition rate

Predation

Plummeting to nadir

Can be ahead of curve in sourcing

Optical illusions

Process alignment – mindset alignment

Energize dreams and not fears

Lean organization that punches well above its weight

Map the world's social terrain in search of its most talented change makers

---

Highly leveraged approach in social change

Recognize wild flowers and help them grow

Bracing for

Attitude decides altitude

Fluid mosaic

People need banking and they may not need Banks
  – Bill Gates

Standard barriers

He is right wing socio path

Actualize dreams

Feet in street

The funds seek to provide social and financial returns to investors

---

Strong and profitable franchise of,,,,

Socially motivated assets

Has ability to use balance sheet to further the field of social finance

---

There is no way to livelihoods
Livelihoods is the only way

Best practices and next practices

Livelihoods is not only income generation but strong convergence

---

All mercy is no justice

World owes no one a living but everyone an opportunity to living
    - Rock Feller

Parochial (narrow)

Clutching to straw

Added to mosaic of nation

Outgrow ego

Desire is getting what you want and satisfaction, is wanting what you got

---

Blunting the momentum

Victory is dependent on who are on your side

Opinion is flexible prejudice

Spiritual without being religion

Top 5 European and bottom 40 sub-Saharan bench mark

Development finance and responsible finance

Fastest inequality in independent India

It is Oracle of our sector

Salaries have gone through the roof but some roofs are collapsible

---

Harsh end poverty

Strike out; do not stop at the third base

Consequence and not process

Predatory commercialization

Today we have more people in offices and business houses than in farms

---

Hedging strategy

Price volatility

Mistaking wood for tree

Potential synergies

Never argue with the person you work for, you will lose more than you argue

---

Every person you meet is your mirror

The "law of the farm" applies to relationships as well as to the rest of life - you reap what you sow and to have great friends you must first be one

---

He is a person with his heart in right place

Be the master of your will but servant of your consciousness

Mental fortitude to disallow worries to come back again and again

---

Work Habits:

Accuracy, efficiency, thoroughness, regularity, timeliness, neatness, orderliness, and punctuality

---

A strong drive for excellence in work product and personal performance

---

When you love what you do no other motivation is necessary

Single source of management services and multilevel technical services

---

Land mark education

Consumed by self image

Tolerance is AC of soul

Stay on purpose and not on outcome

Mind should know that you hold its rein and not vice versa

60/40 rule of listening

Personal light house

As a man thinketh
   – James Allen

Discovering happiness
   - Dennis wholly

Success is not absence of failure

Leader is like conductor of symphony turn back to crowd - satisfaction is output and applause is byproduct

---

Begin with end in mind

Circumstances have converged to create a perfect storm that favored......

Terminable at will

Ultra poverty condition approximates to virtual slavery

We are getting our model together

Endowing the poor with soft and hard resources

Smoothening consumption needs

Building up stake of the poorest

Over bearing agenda

Transformation from funding to lending

Social deprivation harbors in league with economic deprivation

---

Lift the curtain of poverty

Syndrome of collective poverty

Discriminatory net approach

Two way causal relationship

Over exception

Submitting to injustice

In resisting untruth I will put up in all sufferings

Too large for worries

Too noble for anger

Too strong for fear

Too happy to permit trouble

Country has disproportionate share of rain fed areas with dependent populations

---

Non apparent truth

Lack of opportunity and deprivation has locked many of ultra poor in India into deep poverty, blocking them significantly to reach country's booming economy

---

Highly leveraged tool for socio economic change

Process efficiencies

Treat any crisis with Equanimity (composure)

Surviving through a normal life cycle itself is a great challenge

---

The shift from subsistence to market has dramatically negative impact on women

---

75% of income is generated in urban centers

Preserve identity throughout value chain

Orderly transition from ultra poverty

Conversion into member of productive economy

More focus on relevance than excellence

Deeply grounded values and professional ethics

I have looked through many career lenses

It pulled our heart strings to see the pain and misery of the sick and suffering

---

Technical confines

Good are in majority but evil are more organized

Multiple land mark equity

Emotional equilibrium

Emotional vulnerability

Ripple effect

Sweat equity

Overwhelming empirical evidence shows that.............

Mile stones for compensation

Spatial poverty trap

Multi dimensional deprivation

High incidence of people with incomes severely below poverty line

---

Pronounced deprivation

Shooting barbs

Strategy of staying small

Game changers

Inclusive supply/value chains

Soft money

14% of India GDP is going for subsidies

Landlessness is the best predictor of poverty

- Poverty sum total
  a. Income
  b. Calorie
  c. Land
  d. Credit
  e. Nutrition
  f. Health and longevity
  g. Literacy/Female
  h. Safe drinking water
  i. Sanitation
  j. Infrastructure

Gender Work spaces of full breadth philanthropic sector

Effective giving

Impact and solution driven delivery

Seamless and integrated services

Enlightened self interest

Downward movement along with spatial poverty traps

Single source of management and multi level technical services

---

Land mark education

Consumed by self image

Mind should know that you hold its rein not vice versa

One in 8 of the world elderly live in India

Devolve into conduit for subsidies
Evolve into multipurpose rural institutions

Lots of love, light and regards

Customer growth slope is getting steeper

Market penetration of the poor

Personal hero of many of us

Quintessential base of pyramid customers

Deliver broadly on its promise

Within demographics of poor are 5% ultra poor who daily struggle for survival

---

Migration: going in search of less guise possibilities

Indian poor are luckless more than resource less

Well characterized deprivations

Getting act together

Poor suffer from variety of tribulations and afflictions

Core Processes

Direct and indirect correlates

Voicing the voice less

Constructive philanthropy

It is finest approximation we have, to the creative utilization of wealth

---

Giving is inspiring art

Up fronting the poorest

I pray almighty for barter arrangement from God, one year each from our life time could be apportioned to have your endless presence

---

Outliving the utility

Do not save after spending what is left; rather spend what is left after saving

---

Sleeping lobster is carried away by currents

If you buy things you don't need you will be forced to sell things you need

---

Every year adapt couple of old maxims as beacon to guide your future

---

Hands on understanding

Took umbrage (resentment)

Theatre of absurd

Moral sensibility

Intellectual lethargy

A heavy guilt rests upon us

If we do good to poor it is not benevolence but atonement

Gratitude with moderation is idiocracy

For every action there is equal opposite government program

Grand fallacy

If your team is mutual world will be on your finger tips

Poverty: pronounced deprivation in well being

Constructively discontented

To love; to be loved

To never forget your insignificance

To never get used to the unspeakable violence & the vulgar display of life around you

To seek joy in the saddest places

To pursue happiness to its lair

To never simplify what is complicated or complicate what is simple.

To respect strength, never power

Above all to watch

To try and understand

To never look away

And never, never to forget

Creative social entrepreneur willing to engage the very roots of the challenges that characterize a country in often violent transition

---

This person is unflappable and focused

We are at the cusp of the issue

Our Organization unarguably understands best, the requirements as well as complexities involved in the design and implementation of such institutional initiative

---

Celebrate what you have helped achieve the results

Played a script, a cynical and orchestrated one

We can endure neither our condition nor the means to overcome it

---

Back into not so benevolent arms of money lenders

Informal finance rivals if not exceeds the rural banking system

---

Hope this mail will catapult our previous discussions

You can't cross sea by merely staring into water

Worries and tensions are like visiting birds we cannot stop them from flying near us.

But we can certainly stop them from making a nest in our mind

---

A hair cut for both companies and their supporters is must and closeness of the cut is to be decided….

Sticking plaster solutions

Thinking man's game

Relation is not holding hand while you understand each other

It is about having lots of misunderstandings and still not leaving each other

---

Anticipatory and participatory research

As salt in the sea

Pioneering character

A huge thank you to everyone

Relevance and excellence should go hand in hand

Tribal rustic wisdom

I will miss you as colleague but continue to count you as friend

---

We forefeet 3/4th of ourselves in order to be like other people

---

A ticket out of misery

Poverty hovers on outer limits of survival

Beauty of forests fills me with awe and sorrow at the same time

---

Pleasure was all mine

Truths being in and out of favor

Way to resolutions
- Background
- Present status
- Compliance check

- Recommendation
- Resolution

Arbitrary veneration of real above principle

Does not brook an easy solution

Consistency is the last resort of unimaginative

The will to be stupid is very powerful force

Lost its anchor and compass

Torn between opposing ideas and goals

Fixity of purpose

Individual union with God

Metal firmness to restrain from anger

Fertile over heated consciousness

The initiative and its phenomenon is off shoot of extreme poverty

---

Children are caught in their parent's struggle for survival

By undertaking this work you have put us greatly in your debt

---

Government entitlements book

Rapid thinning

God lies in details

We wish you fulfilling Event

Throwing out baby with the bath water

Hunky dory

We understand you are not bound to accept any proposal you receive

---

We take the best of science to solutions

It takes too much energy to be against something unless it is really important

---

Graduation is pointer

Ridiculed by peers when you challenge status quo

Group mentality

Win introduces you to world
Defeat introduces world to you

Agriculture is the only manufacturing process where you buy in retail and sell in wholesale

---

Act like impossible to fail

Who unceasingly takes problems into his hand

Mind is like parachute it works best when opened

Intention is more powerful than intellect

You need iron in your soul to walk through these misery stricken areas

---

Faulty paradigms of development

Entitlement mentality

Deaf people going on unanswering questions that none has asked them

---

Truth stands test of experience

Holding a minute longer

Striking chords

The picture is largely unchanged

But not commensurate with the progress made by the country

Despite stellar growth

Damning evidence

Target determinants of gap than outcomes

Thank you for being part of this journey

Outsized benefits

Rule of thumb training

Weathering bad works

Tribute to his legacy

How the lives of people involved in a program differ from what they would have been like without it

But it is impossible to achieve pure counter factual, the same people the same place but without program

---

Holding with the same reverential awe

In fits and starts

Fossil like seniors

He never misses an opportunity to miss opportunity

Looking forward to professional and mutually fulfilling association

---

Plow to plate

Best of intentions but without best of evidence

Micro canvas and macro canvas

Opportunities of a low carbon economy

I wanted to give my best shot

Scaling up what works

Helping households work out of extreme poverty

Beauty is in the eyes of the beholder

If you owe Rs. 100 it is your problem and if you owe Rs. 10 lakh it is bank's problem

---

World is divided on the basis of what one is born

Chronicle the voice of the voice less

Inextricably linked

Helping vision take shape

It drowns my reasoned voice

Ultra low net worth individuals

Where facts are few experts are many

More to community and less to environment

Impelling vision

Predators sharpening claws

Transparency is competitive advantage

When something is part of infinite it is also infinite

Right of first refusal

Realizing its true place in comity of nations

Now he retires and walks away into sun set

Graduation indicators are guided posters for future livelihoods cycles

---

A bed rock of national economies

Lending the program the common utility character

How much we smile need not depend on how much we earn

Accept past for what it is

Einstein physics but Frankenstein logic

Encourages work - life balance

Broad brush identification of poor as homogeneous entity

Promotional elements and Protective elements

The only maxim of a free government ought to be to trust no man living with power to endanger the public liberty.
— John Adams

The invisible mass

Turn your face to sunlight you will not be able to see shadow

---

Looking at it with renewed eyes

Goes full throttle

Adds to overflowing amount of woes

Cynosure of all eyes

That laid bare the gulf between.......

Future lies with those companies who see poor as their customers

---

To send where it thought belonged – grave yard

What luck for rulers that Men do not think
    – Hitler

Out of 100 biggest economies 51 are corporate

Poor want opportunity not charity

Going to deliver on its promise

Growth slope is getting steeper

Mechanism for slow fade away

It pulls at my heart strings to see

Attainment of fullness

Push factors

You can't go on being a good egg, you hatch or go bad

Be able to stick with a job until it is finished. Be able to bear an injustice without having to get even. Be able to carry money without spending it. Do your duty without being supervised
- Ann Landers

A thing is not necessarily true because man dies for it
- Oscar Wild

It is cause and also consequence

Thin outreach of state services

The turnaround that program brings in is important anchor for broader development

---

Yielding our obligation to...

Living in perpetual denials

Fire up your renewed motivation

Enamored by

For you it is only half a dollar; for us it is 10 reasons to live

---

Widening the exit door

The face of extreme poverty is also gendered

Ultra poor do not move on a linear continuum rather they oscillate in and out of poverty

---

Safety nets, Livelihoods and micro finance are sequenced

We are only as strong as the weakest one amongst us

If it moves tax it
If it still moves regulate it
If it stops subsidize it

Falling between 2 stools

I can't thank you all enough

Weight for weight bamboo is 6 times stronger than iron

Incoherent

The craze has hit a crescendo

Public scrutiny

Steeped in the culture of......

Very down beat about chances of the sector coming back

Non invasive interventions

Survived by skin of his teeth

In negative light

Bellicosity

Ignorance and arrogance combine

Existential threat

The last barrier between death and survival

Law of minimum efforts

If my ears go there first it will be easy to follow it with my body

---

Fear is the mind killer and it is little death

The best way is always through

Our elections are free, only it is in the results where we eventually pay
    - Bill Stern

Rationalized emotions

Promoting measured growth

Wielding a disproportionate degree of influence

Impulse and passion do not co exist with reason

We stay true to our purpose

The greatest tragedy of mankind's entire history is hijacking of morality by religion
    - Arthur C Clarke

Savings is micro capital buffer

Equality of opportunity and not outcome

Geographical band width

It is a case of pot calling the kettle black

Winning combination

Salad days

I respectfully disagree with you

Unapologetically expensive

Seemingly resigned to fact

Poverty and drought merchandize

Goes above head

Selling the soul

Eloquent testimony

Profundity is not strength of teaching

Tie saving discussions

She was everything, the extreme forces stood against

Lied through their teeth

Consistently caught in another deft stick

Dueling narratives

Peddling his own version

Habitual lying

Fringe space

It's like, at the end, there's this surprise quiz: Am I proud of me? I gave my life to become the person I am right now. Was it worth what I paid?
    — Richard Bach

Helped the spark

Vanishing in the thin air

Value systems

Saturate every breath with love

Poverty is unnecessary

Currents and cross currents of strife and struggle

E commerce trends show an exponential growth

Person of steely resilience

Puts on a path of decline abhorrent

A modified variant

Symptomatic of trends and tendencies

Continued to surface periodically

Flies in the face of

Man's capacity for justice makes democracy possible, but man's inclination to injustice makes democracy necessary.
    — Reinhold Niebuhr

Green hypocrite

Put your money where your mouth is

Clout spread

Informed participation

Empirical work on program

It is a strength and not weakness that we are permanently incomplete experiment

---

Context and responsibility allowance

If you share our vision of World without hunger…..

You are up to our challenge

Grant width

The faces of poverty

Be assured, you are helping us make a difference

Program foot print in 2 years

Holding graduation ladder to existing government safety net programs

---

De risking

For the world you may be one person but for one poor person you are the world

---

Turf war

Resource rich but inhabits the poorest

As eye in the time accommodates to darkness

Persistent hungry

Dietary diversity

When you are right you can afford to keep your temper; when you are wrong you can not afford to lose it
   - Mahatma Gandhi

Everything can wait but not agriculture

Break the log jam

Inert facts

SWOCA – strengths, weaknesses, opportunities, challenges and actions

---

Democratic revenge

Matched dollar by dollar

Competitive barriers

Straddling value chain

Saturation appetite

Disintermediation

Empowering farmers in price discovery

Organic farming is blend of philosophy and technology

Organic farming is a process claim and not product claim

Emphasis on on farm management and de emphasis on off farm in puts

---

Irrefutable deductive logic

Income supplement and income replacement

My business would not have been anywhere close to where it is today but for.....

Bone headed leaders

Hydra headed monster............................ poverty

Cut the guardian knot of poverty

Dogma calcified into....

Work is elixir of life

Society that presumes a norm of violence and celebrates aggression, whether in the subway, on the football field, or in the conduct of its business, cannot help making celebrities of the people who would destroy it.
— Lewis H. Lap ham

Having been unable to strengthen justice, we have justified strength.

Raising toast

Information is the currency of the democracy

Summit showdown

One man juggernaut

Diminutive

No tree has branches so foolish to fight amongst themselves

None of is as strong as all of us

Donate eyes, live twice

Plank for financial inclusion

Journey back into time

Pickup in growth has not translated into commensurate decline in poverty

---

First port of call for health related demands and curative needs

---

Poverty – pronounced deprivation in well being

Growth welfare mix

Sitting on blitzkrieg of becoming super star

The cost of staying alive pushes 1/3rd of Ultra Poor into Below Poverty Line

---

Insurance brings the miracles of mathematical probability to the rescue of masses

---

It is doubly ironic that

Has got it so terribly wrong in side its hearth

Process results and substantiative results

Viral market

Savings is infectious

Food security exists when all people at all times have access to sufficient and safe nutritious food to meet their dietary needs and food preference for active and healthy life

---

Had tryst with ignonimity

Inner turmoil of man whose royalty imposes a suffocating weight of expectancy and decorum on a natural and tumultuous king

---

Into cruising mode

Expanding concentric circles of health and awareness around her family

---

We are on the same page

Climbing wrong tree

Schools represent society in microcosm

God is a comedian playing to the audience too afraid to laugh
-Voltaire

Vocational skills, life skills and home skills

Ovarian lottery

My reaction is not guilt but gratitude

We are behind our own success

We expected you to give back in spades but you are coming with spoons

---

I am not made from wood that burns easily

Bouquet of social business

Hybrid organization

Brasington's Ninth Law:

A carelessly planned project takes three times longer to complete than expected; a carefully planned one will take only twice as long.

Community interest companies

Marrying profits to social causes

Impact investment

Ideological progenies of Mahatma Gandhi

Never be too much available for someone, otherwise you will lose importance

---

Self esteem is reputation we acquire with ourselves

The country is cynically manipulating the guilt to further its own unholy ends

---

Surfeit of interplay between main stream investors and social investors

---

Profit maximizing elements tend to trump social indicators

Struggling to keep heads above water

Short straws in the life

Anything else can wait but not ultra poverty

Operational tempo

Make judicious call on to commute to working place

Statistical poverty; destitute poverty

Impact investing sector combining financial return with social and environmental value

---

We can deliver your vision

Working in silos

Pain is fructification of pleasure

Life saving victories against chronic hunger

Big leagues

Learning the long lessons

We are not promising you the world but we are with you

Leading and lagging

Tough innings at the helm

Maharaja of finance is plummeting to bankruptcy

If anybody has to make a thesis on how not to run an organization this is classical case study

---

Epitome of all virtues

It is not what we do, but also what we do not do, for which we are accountable.

Position leader and knowledge leader

Character is destiny

Too much preoccupied with own intellectual

Let him keep me where he loves to keep me

Philanthropic capital

Sharpening of contradictions

Barking wrong trees

Vendetta

Square peg in round hole

Relationship is transactional

Poster boy

Two pillars of micro credit social capital and income generation

---

Not calibrated House hold capacity

Nobody made a greater mistake than he who did nothing

And the day came when the risk it took to remain tight inside the bud was more painful than the risk it took to blossom.

— Anais Nin

Controlled aggression

Working on positives

Long haul of partnership

Double bottom line

Back room bargains

Brand damage

Transactional relationship and not transformational one

We start treating equally but tend to gravitate towards fast climbers

---

Failures are practice shots

I do not feel obliged to believe that the same God who has endowed us with sense, reason, and intellect has intended us to forgo their use.

— Galileo Galilee

Wisdom overweighs any wealth

Teach ideas not facts

In a place where most serious nutrition problem is obesity

- Don't promise when you are happy
- Don't decide when you are sad
- Don't blame when you are angry

Help spot the trends that infringe on…..

Constrained by regulatory procedures

Deceptively simple

Where ideals and pragmatism meet

Responsibly produced

Pragmatic, inspiring and credible ambassadors

Resolute principles

I will never apologize for being me

Providing window of opportunity

A dream worth dreaming

What is point of having a great GDP when as society
we are unhealthy?

Human centered design

Stay meaningful

Mothers' Welfare Index

Sustain the very breath of human race

Never be bullied into silence
Never allow yourself to be made a victim
Accept none's definition of your life
Define yourself

Blind siding

Non-violence leads to the highest ethics, which is the goal of all evolution. Until we stop harming all other living beings, we are still savages.
— Thomas Edison, inventor

Solving wrong problem

Most contemporary and viable solutions

Benefits shared and challenges weathered

Genetic proclivity

Folding the future not extrapolating the past

Seeing wood for tree

Keeping in traction

Intellectual responsibility

My mail indicates my acceptance of agreement

To right the wrong

Harmonizing interests of different stake holders

Future lies with those companies who see poor as their customers

---

Efficiency is intelligent laziness

Established mind set

Thank you ahead of times for any thoughts

We work to deliver standard model

Safety nets are protective and micro finance is promotional

Drives up future costs

Broad brush identification

Poverty program implementation is also political science

Projects with demonstrable societal impact

To keep your spark alive

Continue to carry disproportionate burden of ....

Charity to opportunity

Trade to aid

We plan to drive as much traffic

Emblematic of poverty

World's most intractable challenge

We pioneered the frontiers of global extreme poverty and continue to find solutions

---

Winnow the real from apparent

Back to traction

You have been tying your shoes the wrong way whole of your life

---

Vibrant space in society

Quantitative and qualitative domain experience

It came with whiff of fresh air

Whenever I have a problem, I sing and I realized that my voice is better than the problem

---

It pales in contrast with.............

One who limps is still walking

Double breakeven challenge

Impatient optimists

The crucial disadvantage of aggression, competitiveness, and skepticism as national characteristics is that these qualities cannot be turned off at five o'clock.
— Margaret Halsey

Unearthing dormant forces, faculties and talents

Catching up with the train of globalization

Final piece of puzzle

Non judgmental environment

Building from known to unknown

Repetition aids retention

Don't use your preferred learning style in default training style

---

If you have lived large....

Scarcity mentality and seize mentality

Living in perpetual tornado of noise

There is not any memory with less satisfaction than the memory of some temptation we resisted

---

Great farming casino

Intercrop price parity

There are four ways, and only four ways, in which we have contact with the world. We are evaluated and classified by these four contacts: what we do, how we look, what we say, and how we say it.
    — Dale Carnegie, author and educator

Voice or no voice people can always be brought to the bidding of leaders

---

Listening half, understanding quarter and telling double

Fail; first attempt in learning

Facing a steep learning curve

Idiot proof process

Small ticket and high ticket

Calibrated to supply and not demand

Lifestyle choice

Biologically dictated birth

Feeding frenzy

Worshipping market & Respecting market

Only way we cross desert is through it

It is dangerous to be right when government is wrong
  - Voltaire

Alter ego

Pontification

Manifestation of perverted mind

Takes gloves off on…..

Weaving livelihoods around micro finance

Cruelest form of inequity and social exclusion

Deliver as one approach

Future belongs to nations with grains and not guns

Cold as ice on outside but has fire in the heart

God gives everybody food but he doesn't not throw into nest

Private sector flexibility; public sector scale

Game changing innovations

Focusing tool

Responsibilities are included but not restricted to

Poster child

For all our conceits about being the center of the universe, we live in a routine planet of a humdrum star stuck away in an obscure corner ... on an unexceptional galaxy which is one of about 100 billion galaxies. ... That is the fundamental fact of the universe we inhabit, and it is very good for us to understand that.
   — Carl Sagan

Whipped up themselves into frenzy

The crisis of child under nutrition that leads to denial even at birth of the opportunity for full expression of a child innate genetic potential for physical and mental development

---

Bearing torch in heart

Livelihoods unfolding

Marble floor lobby

Compassion cannot be taught

He got earful from his boss

Unconditional acceptance

Love people and use things
Use people and love things

To handle yourself use your head
To handle others use your heart

Everyone has photographic memory, some don't have film

Burn the night

Commercial cost savvy

We must be the change we want to see

Love is so close, that there is no space for two

Saving grace

Iron inside the will

Unfailingly reliable

She defeats her discomfort....

When you are done to nothing
God is there up to something

Bad apple

Throwing baby out of bathwater

She lost him but found herself and some that was everything

I write because I don't know what I say until I read what I say

---

Always trade within your limit position

World is teetering on the edge of another recession

Over prepare

Important sex organ is brain

Share a spoon with them

Deep dive

It is my DNA

Longitudinal study

Angered grief

His creation of purely abstract work followed a long period of development and maturation of intense theoretical thought based on his personal artistic experiences, shapes, colors, lines, and use of space always express the reality found in nature, but its structure rather than its appearance.

Intense spirit

Recharging emotional batteries

Heart has its own reason

In conflict would you stay with your heart or fly with your mind

---

Oppose when in opposition
Propose when in position

Deep down we are all part of cosmic joke

Loss is not defeat quit is

Eco profits

Judge people by distance travelled not by their peak of excellence

---

Never wound what u can't kill

Lived through the pain of --------

Mobilization of hope

The most consistent finding in our work is heightened level of creativity

---

Gravity that we have created…………...

The idea has muscle

He has muscle and can pull heavy weights

I have been muscled out to secure …….

Always a pleasure to hear from you

The entire intellectual edifice has collapsed

Unguarded honesty

Right makes might not the other way round

Wears you out to depths of Soul

The system robs of hope

Real power has heart

Calamitous lapse of judgment

Completely drained of all emotions

I have nothing but respect for you

Faceless cog in the machinery of ....

Bring humanity to work

Bring my best self to your market place and be rewarded for it

---

Over stayed his welcome

Turning Nelson's eye

Our common thread is.... .....

We are a success-driven consulting firm in the business of transforming companies.

We will work with you to expand your Brand's footprint across India and worldwide

---

We will create a comprehensive success blueprint to move your company's performance from where it currently stands to where it has the potential to go

---

We aim to catapult your company into an auto-pilot success mode by transferring our skills to your staff

---

Our USP is in transferring our long years of expertise to client for speedy, best return on investment

---

Dynamic mosaic

Fear of unknown has built faith

Reverse of Mida's touch

We solicit your engagement in the process of building a new paradigm that allow us to use our rich bio diverse resource that secures intergenerational stake

---

Genetic high way

Ecology Economy Equity

Love me the way I am

Twisted mind set

Utilize -- strengths

Manage --- weaknesses

Advantage of opportunities

Minimize impact of threats

Patriotism is verb not noun

Generational poverty

Passionate social agenda

It is not the strongest of the species that survives nor the most intelligent, but the one most responsive to change
   – Charles Darwin

Aggressive and diligent

Polite argument

Financial foot prints

Honest difference of opinion on debate is not disunity

Knock the bottom out of

Organization as problem rather than anchor

Politics has no space for losers

Ali and coolie

Pulling out all stops to give aid

Dark under belly

Alter ego

Wearing compassion on sleeve

Courage of conviction

Basic survival

Dysfunctional people

Latent terror infrastructure that can be potentiated with right political eco-system

---

Live in your story

Radical self care

Mental resiliency

A boat is safe in the harbor but that is not the purpose
of boat

Don't allow your wounds to transform you into some
you are not

Necessary and unnecessary enemies

Hyphen between ruin and life

Please contact me if there is anything else I can do

Running out of nouns

Staying rooted to core values

There is manifest need

Charisma and enigma

If you are failing to prepare you should be prepared to fail

Humanity is becoming giraffe with distance growing between brain and heart

---

Spiritual home of ….

Nobody can break egg and sperm

Eye ball brand recall

Fizzle out

Status ideologue

I am nothing if not a team player

Not a patented issue to anybody

Going above and beyond role

Negative engagement

Hitting nail on head

To improve is change and to excel is changing constantly

Faithful dissenter

Please help us understand to serve better

Negative engagement

Reverse coping mechanism

Battle against fate

Hankering back to failed systems

How much easy to be critical than correct

Emotional intensity

Karmic commitment

Justice is surrendered to appeasement

Manifestly dishonest

Extenuating circumstance

Democracy ensures we shall be groomed no better than we deserve

---

Surrounded by wrong people

Organization is not a commodity belonging to you
It is a system to which we all belong

What matters more design, mentoring and market support

Include but not limited

Demonstrable impact

Life is never linear

Addressing multitude of vulnerabilities

Breaking margins

Working in unfair constraints

Arbitrage opportunities

Recruit on potential – reward on performance

Upping the decibel level

Responding directly to the needs of the poorest and most vulnerable

---

Underserved communities to improve life supporting initiatives that lead to developing sustainable outcomes through scale

---

Resource limited circumstance

Dissemination model

Evidence based training

Markets aggregate preference without judging them

Deeper appeal

There is space for eminence but not for pre-eminence

Moral limits of markets

Value neutral

Its thinking is rooted in partition

He seems to have bent so many times, he looks prostrate

Brighter part of disappointment

It's his run in the Sun

Alchemizing poverty to sustainability

Unhinged principle verticals

You have chosen the side of oppressor

To believe in something and not to live it is dishonest
- Mahatma Gandhi

Crushing poverty

None can destroy iron but its own rust; so is our mind set

Has shown himself to be consummate scientist and engineer, beholder to evidence and committed to upholding the highest scientific standards

---

He has also done his part to make sure the people benefit from advances in technology

---

Ground breaking ideas to market

Opportunity to engage in ground action research

Inflation is income tax on poor

Touching crescendo

We can't emphasize enough how important it is

How to pull from its black hole of technology

Remote low resource villages

I have been stymied in my further attempts to scale this project by lack of funding support

---

If there are any synergies with your work I would be delighted to explore how we could work together

---

Religion is the last refuge of human slavery

They fought and died for it; but never lived it

Cultivated as equalizer

Head at heart regime

Non-Profit head regime
Corporate ROI regime

On the ground solutions for enhancing incomes of the underprivileged

---

Social maximizing, surplus generating, non dividend paying company

---

Re payable if and when basis

Social Return on Investment

Multi optimization on dimensions of people, planet and profit

---

Business competence with social passion

Traveler like attitude: plan well but be flexible to adapt, focused on end but enjoy journey

---

Make it happen spirit

Rhetoric tactics

It prides itself

Women are at the centre of our organization's effort to defeat poverty and we found they often make the best entrepreneurs

---

In the business of creating opportunities for the poor

A sector most unfairly maligned in India

Demanding perfectionist

Our Organization's signature endeavor program is,,,,,,

Poverty is the most pressing challenge facing the planet

Succession pictures

Become a better version of yourself

Impact on especially, marginalized communities

Green shoots emerging

Thank you for writing our success story

India needs social business for true inclusion

Return of capital rather than return on capital

The way we think about charity is dead wrong

Staggeringly on target analysis

Ethical road blocks

Lean euphemism for totally under resourced

Frugality Vs morality

Inefficient way to become wealthy

Getting anchored

Beating the odds

Running away from problem increases distance from solution

For profit counter intuitive proposition

Dare the world to save planet

I am still under weather......

I need my space as much you need yours.
Conflict arises when your path crosses mine

Uncertainty impels man to unfold his power

I will go ballistic...

Don't hit at all if it is possible to avoid hitting; but never hit softly

Journalists should talk to people not talk at people

India's ignored hinterlands

Marshall Resources and support

Buried in work

Optimize pitch for their funders

Rebranding

Equitable apportionment

To drive triple bottom line performance

I am in for the long haul

Stop trying to fit in when you were born to stand out

His greed is taking toll on every program

Best way to talk to is to listen

Boredom and fear, the latter being the heavier cross

A fallow mind becomes over grown with weeds of confusion and forgetfulness

---

Committed heart with trained rational mind

Counter weight

Be thankful for difficult people in my life for they have shown me who I do not want to be

---

I will miss you until next time

Radical Islam has today charted a path that mirrors radical capitalism, using violence only shocks "us" because we've managed to make the violence unleashed and supported for so long in our name morally and politically invisible. The major world powers have long coddled favored local despots of whatever ideological stripe. But the strength of the relationships between western governments and the petroleum-rich states of the Arab world, secured by trillions of dollars cycling back and forth between them through oil and arms sales, finance and heavy industry, is historically unprecedented.

Helping to ensure consistency and equity

Talk to each other and not talk about each other

Evaluate then promote, demote or terminate

Inner peace is not allowing others to control our emotions

Suboptimal yet sustainable solutions

Economically driven pursuit

The Organization is about thresholds not maximization

Markets are internally focused and surpluses appropriately enter external markets not the reverse

---

Not disparate economic solutions but integrated options

Greedy indiscretion

Baby step

Eat crow

It is not just what he has done for firm externally; but his personal conviction on the importance of human resources have resonated the company

---

Multiple bottom line returns

We wish to dive deeper

Scaling collective hypothesis

Industry is at an inflection point

We are sitting only with right ingredients but without recipe

---

Clarion call for action

Course correction

Bio available

Education is not for mere living;. Again, education is not for developing the faculty of argument, criticism, or winning a polemic victory over your opponents or exhibiting your mastery over language or logic; it is for life, a fuller life, a more meaningful, a more worthwhile life

---

In a furrow

Default victim

Setback to comeback

Creating de-motivating climate

Creating an effective pitch on…...

In an ideal world they would throw themselves into creating a thoughtful specific constructive review

---

My way or highway

The reality slowly dawned on them

To suit political prejudices

Score cards for strategy execution

Hold public office for personal aggrandizement

Classic paranoia of despot

Build personal wealth on public money

Opened window to see wonderful meadow

Good is enemy of the best

Cherry pitch

Life saving diagnosis test

Leveraging business for social change

I will endeavor to deal with all the outstanding issues as soon as possible

---

Solar soldiers empowers women with economic opportunity and access to technology using social business model for clean energy products. We combine break through potential of affordable solar energy with deliberately women centered direct sales net work to bring light, hope and opportunity to tribals

---

Energy poverty to economic opportunity

Negative internalities and positive externalities

Hitting hard patch

As the world confronts paradigm shift in sector

Shaping contemporary society

Research on global scale and across generations

Negative legacy

Richness is ability to share not hoard

Crowd funding

Green loans

Innovative view points from which to put up sign posts leading to new era

---

Positive ripple effects

Head space

Taking wind out of sail

Investors zero in on gold as hedge

In a vortex of crushing poverty

Herd behavior

Status quo thinking and compartmentalized expertise

Global scale

Lowering the demand curve

Bio diversity hot spots

C 4 approach
- Conservation
- Cultivation
- Consumptions
- Commerce

- Rare Endemic Threatened (RET) plant diversity
- Community managed gene, seed, and grain and water banks

- Genetic literacy
- Documentation of local conservation traditions
- Ex-situ genetic conservation center
- Repository of various genetic stocks
- Living gene banks
- Chronicling of dying wisdom

Participatory societal purification

Conservation and commercialization are mutually reinforcing

Diet survey

Shadow recruit

Food security – availability, absorption and access

Analytical separation of extreme poverty from general poverty into 3 dimensions of Food security, Livelihoods and Capacity building helps in policy framing

---

Leap frog into center stage of global business

Identity based barriers

Program Design principles

- Inclusion
- Scalability
- Sustainability
- Replicability
- Innovation
- Growth potential

Enjoy facilitating teams to be entrepreneurial and leap boundaries

---

Applying innovation to responsibly leverage base of pyramid opportunities in emerging markets

---

Underserved markets in emerging economies

Scale aspirations

Never judge what you don't understand

Public Relationship bullet

Poster child

Bucket list

On the cusp of recession

Building resilience in communities

Debt counseling for clients

Speaking through the hat

Conservation and commercialization are mutually reinforcing

To wear purple

Frame every disaster - in 5 years will this matter?

Men of straw

Never ration appreciation

Even your shadow leaves you when you are in darkness

Words can hardly express my grief at the news

Malleable

We have strength to stare it down

It has grown beyond conceptual stage and has demonstrated impact and sustainability

---

Shape the emergent economy with your solution and thinking

Most current and compelling version of your pitch for social change

---

Your personality should shine through

Project ingredients
- Pitch
- Problem
- Solution
- Example
- Impact
- Market place
- Sustainability
- Team

Sector pandemic

Cultivate solidarity through psycho social groups

Diapers and Politicians need to be changed often and for the same reason

---

Failing to show spine

Please give us benefit of your valuable presence and guidance

---

Birds born in cage think flying is weakness

Comparative advantage

Her confidence comes in part from knowing she has some one from her own community who she trusts to walk her through

---

Hegemony

In extricate link

Essential nutrient in our life is to have contact with other living beings.

Stop being pain in the neck

With our backs against the wall we have to do everything possible

---

Deeper reflection is needed

Breaking open the front door

Good Introduction to a Project (example)

The CGAP-Ford Foundation Graduation Program is a global effort to understand how safety nets, livelihoods and access to finance can be sequenced to create sustainable pathways for the poorest out of extreme poverty and into sustainable livelihoods. Since 2006, the Graduation Program has partnered with local organizations and governments to adapt the approach in 10 pilot projects in eight countries. A unique element of the Graduation Program is that a robust learning and evaluation agenda, including qualitative research and randomized controlled evaluations, is embedded in all the pilot sites.

We must, however, acknowledge, as it seems to me, that man with all his noble qualities...still bears in his bodily frame the indelible stamp of his lowly origin.
 - Charles Darwin

Proprietary arrogance

Incubator of entrepreneurial process

Harsh words burn to ash

Urban farming remained creating large scale distribution opportunities for micro sized farms

---

We are out to prove it

Setting global example

Engage and include communities into value chains and markets in a sustainable and equitable way

---

Promoting "Info Lady"

Searching for approaches

Caption of a solar project
"Give her solar wings to soar high"

Social sector and business can co-exist

Redrawing the boundaries

Bureaucracy is corrosive institution

Life is under no obligation to give us what we expect

To strengthen change makers as an eco system that supports growth of your innovation

---

Feelings are like waves you can't stop but can choose which one to surf

---

Board room gorilla and white collar gorilla

Fallacious

Cats amongst pigeons

Pursue like young and relate like grown up

He is kicking in the head of ….…..because he can

Conquering expectations

Cross cutting theme of gender and social exclusion

Trying to fit in when born to stand out

Ties outweigh squabbles

Empowered and employable

Debate on emotions rather than reasons

Intellectual mafia

You should commit them to your very soul

That fits into business paradigm

Massive congratulations

Exercised deep emotional control

Today we have had our brush with history

Intense friendship

Life variable width, depth and length, the last is the only one not in your hand

---

Softening the fiber

A nation need not be cruel to be tough

Critical scale mile stones

GPS indicators to identify its location

Sometimes peace is better than being right

Working beyond the call of duty

Taking up negative space of mind

Your patience
When you have nothing
Attitude when you have everything

It is deep and continuing need

Self sustaining bottom up distribution net works

Natural inclination to be a follower and not leader

Merit and integrity have no value and we continue to sink beneath suffocating weight of rampant greed

---

Ethical lapse

Our common thread is language

He has nothing to keep bones

Barren skepticism

We are all prisoners of our own passion

Explosive gamble

Championing equity

Critical thinking and preparation

That embodies finest dreams our founding fathers had envisaged for us

---

He uses Trust proxies to calibrate Trust spending

Autonomy of my conscience

Overwhelming nonsense

Transcend to human boundaries

Turning Nelson's eye

Overstayed his welcome

Bring my best self to your market place and be rewarded by it

---

Faceless cog in the machinery of organization

I have nothing but respect for you

Completely drained of all emotions

Calamitous lapse of judgment

Real power has heart

Never wound what you really can't kill

Lived through the pain of……..

Mobilization of hope

The most consistent finding in our work is heightened level of creativity

---

Gravity that you have created

In the organization he has muscle and can pull weights

Unfortunately you are on the wrong side of logic

The two trajectories are rooted in bad policy

We are entitled for some mistakes in life

Professional courtesy

Over whelming nonsense

Transcend to human boundaries

I am declaring autonomy of my consciousness

Championing enquiry, critical thinking and preparation

We are prisoners of our own passion

Barren skepticism

He has nothing to keep honest

Our common thread is ....

Personal speed bumps

I had different spin

Monumental fraud

Flash point

Suffering from inbreeding depression as you are refusing to learn from ground

---

How nicely written inviting a proposal

Impact on the poor: Does the proposal clearly identify the targeted beneficiaries and articulate what will change for them? Is there a clear connection between the stated objectives and the proposed impact on the lives of the targeted marginalized population?

- **Demonstrated results**: Has the business model been operational for at least two years? Is the provider able to demonstrate a track record of successful project implementation?

- **Operational readiness**: Is the implementation time frame and budget realistic? Does the organization have the capacity needed to implement the project?

- **Potential for growth and large scale impact**: Is there potential for expansion? How will grant participation help the provider achieve large scale impact beyond the grant period? Can the project be replicated elsewhere?

- **Financial sustainability**: How will the organization use the grant to build a pathway for financial self-sufficiency? Does the project have the potential to be financially sustainable beyond funding?

- **Business model innovation**: How does the proposed approach represent a novel solution for solving critical challenges in the target states?

Companies have battle grounds very clear; they have a "day bread" kind of fights in market place

---

Deep value

Except for good, our voice should never be heard

You don't have to choose between

Making a living and making a difference

Barricades of ideas are worth more than barricades of stones

"From the perspective of our ranking criteria — impact, innovation and sustainability —the organization ticks every box," wrote the development magazine

---

DHAKA, Bangladesh -

From its blood-soaked war of independence from Pakistan 42 years ago to disasters — natural and industrial — Bangladesh has long been known for epic human suffering and poverty

It has come to be known for social innovations that have attacked its myriad problems with some impressive successes

---

I give him all kudos for doing that

He enjoys rock star status from College campuses to Capitol Hill

---

The real miracle of organization is that it remains nimble and responsive despite its size

---

Navigating the thick grey zone

I am very proud of my association with .... which is doing good work in often difficult circumstances and making an extraordinary difference to millions of lives. My own professional activities take me to developing countries in all continents, thus I can offer the global view that good organizations are built, as is ...... through a credible commitment to values and relentless focus on innovating and realizing efficiencies. ....is right amongst the top few in a list of great organizations. Its effect is already being felt worldwide

---

Infectious enthusiasm

Government ....whole sale

Community Based Organization ....retail

Social mobilization to Institution building to financial inclusion to sustainable livelihoods

---

Training focus to retention focus

It is important to remember that just as our words are our thoughts

---

Verbalized, to our deeds are our beliefs actualized,. No action, no matter how small is insignificant – how we treat someone defines how we treat everyone including ourselves. If we disrespect another we disrespect ourselves. If we are mistrustful of others we are distrustful of ourselves. If we can't appreciate those around we can't appreciate our selves. With every person we engage, in everything we do we must be kinder that expected more generous than anticipated, more positive than we thought possible. Every moment in front of another human being is an opportunity to express our highest values and to influence someone with other humanity. We can make the world better, one person at a time
   - Robin Sharma

Horizon scanning to spot development trends

Neo-liberalism and jihadist are in fact happy bedfellows (the famous Charlie Hebdo cover of an Islamist and a secular Frenchman kissing would have more accurately depicted a banker, not a hipster.)Both are rapidly anti-democratic, support the concentration of wealth and power, and draw much of their strength from violence, war and a manageable level of chaos that keep oil prices high and petrodollars recycled via everything from fancy weapons to even fancier real estate.

Early signals

Unique position at the intersection of social and commercial business sectors

---

"More than money" approach

PLATONIC love is like being invited down to the wine cellar for a glass of soda

---

THE TOUGHEST part of dieting isn't watching what you eat—it's watching what your friends eat

---

MONEY isn't everything, according to those who have it

Deep sourcing of impact investors

It's my pleasure knowing you

Moral limit of markets

Inter generational stake

Passionate social agenda

Insulating from contagion risk

Embraces market principles while pursuing a social objective

That would entail generation, harvest, documentation, cross fertilization, use of innovative knowledge processes and products

---

I am sending a big hug your way

King of wishful thinking

Horizontally differentiated banking systems
Virtually differentiated banking systems

Dependent on the munificence of State

Running rough shod over basic human rights

Has gone over board

Trust in God but lock your car

Flaunt Ads

ALBERT EINSTEIN:

The Prussian Academy of Sciences is a fast-track academic institute that requires a proactive, hands-on-type individual to overthrow the Newtonian conception of the universe. The successful candidate will have an excellent command of mass, energy, space, time and some maths. Bonus paid upon completion of proofs. Skills in LIGO preferred.

WINSTON CHURCHILL:

Are you an action-oriented, take-charge person interested in exciting new challenges? As director of a major public-sector organization, you will manage a large armed division and interface with other senior executives in a team-oriented, multinational initiative in the global marketplace. Successful candidate will have above-average oral-presentation skills.

CHRISTOPHER COLUMBUS:

Dynamic, rapidly expanding European monarchy seeks a can-do visionary to head up its South American divisions. Our ideal candidate will have at least five years' experience in New World colonization and be willing to accept shift work. Fluency in Spanish an asset. Some travel involved.

MICHELANGELO:

Lorenzo de' Medici seeks highly skilled, aesthetically oriented individual to conceive and implement several major public projects. You are a generalist with sound training in structural engineering, synthesis of pigments and Christian iconography. Some climbing involved.

Private rate of return and social rate of return

He combined – years of living at work at the grass roots with academic research and policy deeply informed by his endeavors in the field

---

Gap between outlays and outcomes

File based transfer to real time transfer

Disrupting status quo and driving large change

Living on base subsistence

Empowerment gap

Losing the double income edge

I am enough of a realist and more of an optimist

Social Enterprise organization that uses business methods to achieve social or environmental mission that serves the under privileged communities

---

Impact investors

YOU DO have to admire one thing about TV serial families – they never waste time watching television

---

People should attain more economically empowered life

Financial thought crime

Worldly advice

GOD SAVE you from a bad neighbor and from a beginner on the fiddle
    – Italian Proverb.

BEFORE YOU marry, keep your two eyes open; after you marry, shut one.
- Jamaican Proverb.

IF YOU want your dreams to come true; don't sleep
— Yiddish Proverb

FAULTS ARE thick where love is thin.
— British Proverb

WITH TIME and patience the mulberry leaf becomes a silk gown.
- Chinese Proverb

TREAT your guest as a guest for two days, on the third day; give him a hoe.
- Swahili Proverb.

Kowtow (be conventional)

Work place misfits

Unpleasant mismatch of economic and social development

The health care jigsaw cuts across quality of care and rural and urban divide

---

That can bring about orbit shift

Delinking poverty line from entitlements

Program specific indicators vis-à-vis entitlements

Universal Indicators and deprivation specific indicators

Trouble is inevitable but suffering is optional

It becomes more satisfying to help entrepreneurs than to be one.

My ignorance is just as good as your knowledge

There is syndrome in business called paralysis by analysis

Capacity to work without extensive direction

Most people live and die with their music still unplayed, they never dare to try

---

Diplomacy is art of diving into troubled water without making splash

---

Expected to shape world events

Subtlety is saying what you think and getting out of range before it is understood

Heavy hitter

Its house of failure built on nails of excuses

Head and shoulders above the competition

But in the 21st, 15th or 57th century - whatever your religion, calendar, or country - there is no excuse or justification for responding to art with murder. But there is a clear and frightening explanation for this violence, one that demands not merely outrage at the act itself, but at the system that has made it both predictable and inevitable. The problem is that this system is hundreds of years old, implicates most everyone, and has only become more entrenched in the last several decades as the world has become ever more globalised.

Comfort of opinion is not superior to discomfort of thought

Am I not destroying enemies when I make them friends?

Reside outside your body

Their combination made for a deadly cocktail that almost killed Organization

---

Riding the tiger that he can never tame

Flash point

She has buried so much of pain and bitterness in her heart

Helping make informed livelihoods choices

One regret in my life is that I am not someone else

Friction free implementation

Vogue outside and vague inside

Multi input development program

The easy way to make God laugh is to tell him about your plans

---

Everything else is just details

Everyone has an invisible sign hanging from their neck saying, 'Make me feel important.' Never forget this message when working with people.
   - Mary Kay Ash

Keeping his powders dry

Anthropogenic green house gas emissions

Glow and glare

Resistance to change is endemic

He laid an exaggerated stress on not changing one's mind

NOSTALGIA is like sex; every generation thinks it is discovering it for the first time.

Matrixed leadership group

These pilots are also expected to generate evidence on the kinds of design that will be needed to ensure effective delivery of appropriate systems

---

Strong sense of ownership with every deliverable

We are super glad

Everybody is genius but if you judge a fish by its ability to climb a tree it will live its whole life believing that it is stupid

---

Closing the loop

It helps gain edge in winning

Grass roots immersion with socially excluded communities

Design principles of program
- Scalability
- Inclusion
- Sustainability
- Replicability
- Innovation
- Growth potential

While mind gets smaller the audience get bigger

Personal speed bumps

The framers of the Indian Constitution articulated a future of India as an enlightened society of free citizens, where diversity among our people was celebrated, where no monochromatic ideology could reign and where the creative impulses of people living in a shared space would take India to the front ranks of the modern world

---

I had different spin

Monumental fraud

Making markets work for poor

We advocate paradigm shift in the treatment of work from a post facto accounting to a pro active need based demand driven planning process with stringent appraisal approval, monitoring and evaluation mechanism

---

Accelerator services

The two trajectories are rooted in bad policy

We are all entitled for some mistakes in life

Professional courtesy

There are worse things in life than death. Have you ever spent an evening with an insurance salesman?
  - Woody Allen

Overwhelming nonsense

Transcend to human boundaries

I am dealing with autonomy of my conscience

He used organizational proxies to calibrate spending

Power always thinks it has a great soul and vast views beyond the comprehension of the weak.

Championing enquiry, critical thinking and preparation

Completely drained off all emotions

Calamitous lapse of judgment

Indeed, the chances of healing - of some level of local, democratically accountable control of political and economic development - have become even more remote in the era of neoliberal globalization, which has been rightly seen by many across the region as essentially colonialism dressed in new clothes (IMF and World Bank policies strongly resemble those of the international banks that brought Tunisia, Egypt and the Ottoman Empire to bankruptcy, and ultimately foreign control, between 1863 and 1875)

Real power has heart

The most consistent finding in our work is heightened level of creativity

---

Gravity that you have created

Unfortunately you are on the wrong side of logic

You are needlessly burning your bridges

You are desirous of wealth which is not yours

Hurry sickness

Behind the veneer of public service there is attempt to reap rich harvest in the name of welfare

---

He has nothing to keep honest

The general population doesn't know what is happening and it even doesn't know that it doesn't know

---

We are all prisoners of our own passion

Championing enquiry

Critical thinking and preparation

That embodies finest dreams our founding fathers have envisaged for us

---

Explosive gamble

Autonomy of conscience

You've got to date a lot of Volkswagens before you get to your Porsche
   - DEBBY ATKINSON

Overwhelming non sense

Patriotism cannot be our final spiritual shelter, my refuge is humanity

---

The establishment has incrementally lost its collective mind over the issue

---

Warning –

Going to sleep on Sunday

Will cause Monday

I could not be less interested in cars if I took a pill to achieve it

---

Transcend to human boundaries

Professional courtesy

Air of make believe

Bring my best self to your market place and be rewarded for it

---

Faceless cog in the machinery of Organization

If you try and take a cat apart to see how it works, the first thing you have on your hands is a non-working cat.

I have nothing but respect for you

Working beyond call of duty

Taking up negative space of mind

Have patience when you have nothing
Attitude when you have everything

There is deep and continuing need

Self sustaining bottom up distribution net work

Natural inclination to be follower than leader

Everybody, no matter how old you are, is around 24, 25 in their heart
    - BRUCE WILLIS

Merit and integrity have no value and we continue to sink beneath the suffocating weight of rampant greed

---

Ethical lapse

Love is over rated, bio chemically it is not greater than eating large chocolate

---

For a merchant even honesty is financial speculation

Wearing an invisible crown

While the mind gets smaller the audience gets bigger

Ties outweigh squabbles

For a moment, nothing happened. Then, after a second or so, nothing continued to happen
  - A screen play narrative

Empowered and employable debate on emotions rather than reasons

---

Intellectual mafia

You should commit them to your very soul

What holds us back in life is the invisible architecture of fear. It keeps us in our comfort zones, which are, in truth, the least safe places in which to live. Indeed the greatest risk in life is, taking no risks,. But every time we do that which we fear, we take back the power that fear has stolen from us. - For on the other side of our fears live our strengths. Every time we step into the discomfort of progress and growth we become freer. The more fears we walk through the more power we reclaim. In this way we grow both fearless and powerful and thus are able to live the lives of our dreams.

   - Robin Sharma

That won't fit into business paradigm

Massive congratulations

Exercised deep emotional control

Today we have had our brush with history

Intense friendship

Life variable width, depth and length
The last is the only one not in your control

Sometimes peace is better than being right

Auto pilot mode

Critical scale mile stones

A common mistake that people make when trying
to design something completely foolproof is to
underestimate the ingenuity of complete fools

A nation need not be cruel to be tough

Softening the fiber

Give her wings to soar high

Bureaucracy – corrosive institution

Life is under no obligation to give us what we expect

To strengthen change makers as an eco system that support growth of your innovations

---

Feelings are like waves you can't stop but can choose which one to surf

---

Board room gorilla

White collar gorilla

Fallacious

Cats amongst pigeons

Pursue like young and relate like grown up

He is kicking in the head of organization because he can

Conquering expectations

Cross cutting theme of gender and social exclusion

Trying to fit in when born to stand out

Corruption + arrogance = corrugance

In extricable link

Stop being pain in the neck

Human beings, who are almost unique in having the ability to learn from the experience of others, are also remarkable for their apparent disinclination to do so

--Douglas Adams

With our backs against the wall we have to do everything possible

---

Deeper reflection

Breaking open the front door

Radical departure

Proprietary arrogance

Incubator of entrepreneurial prowess

Harsh words burn to ashes

Creating large scale distribution opportunities for micro sized farms

---

Engage and include communities into value chains and markets in a sustainable and equitable way

---

Most compelling and current version of your pitch for social change

---

Your personality should shine through….

Your analysis of any topic

> Pitch
> Problem solution
> Example
> Impact
> Market place

Sector pandemic

Cultivate solidarity through psycho social groups

Failing to show spine

Lash of wit

Please give us benefit of your valuable presence and guidance

---

Her confidence comes in part from knowing she has some one from her own community who she trusts to walk her through Graduation from extreme poverty

---

Seductive promises

Speaking through the hat

Conservation and commercialization are mutually reinforcing

To wear purple

Frame every disaster – in 5 years will this matter?

Don't audit life

Don't ration appreciation

Malleable

We have strength to stare it down

It has grown beyond conceptual stage and has demonstrated impact and sustainability

---

Your limit is our limit

20% consume 80% and poorest 20% consume only 1.3%

Transactional and Transformational interventions

Climate smart agriculture

Credit appetite

Controlling opportunistic approach

For the purpose of economics village is my world, for the purpose of culture world is my village

---

Gendered value chain

The Boarding on Flight ✈ 20... has been announced.......
Your luggage should only contain the best souvenirs from 2015..... The bad and sad moments should be left in the garbage.......

The duration of the flight will be 12 months

So, tighten your seatbelt

The next stop-over will be: Health, Love, Joy, Harmony, well-being and Peace

The captain offers you the following menu which will be served during the flight.......

- A Cocktail of Friendship
- A Supreme of Health
- A Gratin of Prosperity
- A Bowl of Excellent News
- A salad of Success
- A Cake of Happiness

Let Me Thank All The Good People Like You

Who made the year 20…. Beautiful for Me

Eagles fly above clouds to avoid rain

Extordinary determination in the face of adversity

Wearing the borrowed coat

Stickiness in business

The compelling motivation for me to get up and work every day is to make sure that development reaches all

---

Rainbow nation

Be nice to people on your way up because you may meet them on your way down

---

Champions among learners should be regarded as resource

Lofty rhetoric

I won't give you the gift of hating you. You want it, but to respond to hatred with anger would be to give in to the same ignorance that made you what you are. If this God for whom you kill blindly made us in his image, every bullet in the body of my wife is a wound in his heart. You would like me to be scared, for me to look at my fellow citizens with a suspicious eye, for me to sacrifice my liberty for my security. You have lost. I saw her this morning. At last, after nights and days of waiting. She was as beautiful as when she left on Friday evening, as beautiful as when I fell head over heels in love with her more than 12 years ago.

Us two, my son and I, we will be stronger than every army in the world. I cannot waste any more time on you as I must go back to [my son] who has just woken from his sleep. He is only just 17 months old, he is going to eat his snack just like every other day, then we are going to play like every other day and all his life this little boy will be happy and free. Because you will never have his hatred either."

--Antoine Leiris, bereaved husband of a young woman killed in Paris attack

---

An exuberant explosion of blissfulness

"Of course I am devastated with grief, I grant you this small victory, but it will be short-lived. I know she will be with us every day and we will find each other in heaven with free souls which you will never have"

Keep your friends close; and your enemies closer

Someone with seasoning subtlety and sophistication

Tied umbilically

Collective wound

Lawyers can steal more money with a briefcase than a thousand men with guns and masks

---

The collective wound of colonialism, its distortion and often destruction of existing pathways to modernity, is for all practical purposes immeasurable. As with a body that takes only seconds to stab or shoot, the deep wounds of foreign domination and postcolonial dictatorship can take a lifetime to heal properly, if ever.

Laws are always like spider webs, weak and small get caught, but powerful hawks torn them away

---

Scourge of nihilistic terror.

If Charlie Hebdo reminds us of anything it is that the arc of blowback can stretch for decades, growing more uncontrollable as the political, economic, social and technological chaos of the contemporary world increases.

A block of sweet, when cut into three equal pieces has the same sweetness, weight and shape. The three attributes cannot be separated as we do not find sweetness in one part, weight in another and shape in the third part. When the sweet is placed on the tongue and it starts to melt, the taste is recognized, weight is lessened and shape modified simultaneously. So too, the *Jiva* (individual) and the *Paramatma* (God) are not separate. They are one and the same. Therefore, each act you undertake must be in the spirit of service, love and wisdom. This is verily the roadmap to reach God. -

---

Inner engineering

We are problem for ourselves

Well behaved women never make history

Blaming your faults on your nature does not change the nature of your faults

---

I am goanna get medieval on your ass

To attain knowledge, add things every day. To attain wisdom, remove things every day
    – LAO TZU

Psychological mile stone

Everyone makes and carries within him his own "heaven" or "hell", and you don't need to die to go there

---

In the middle of ship wreck

Tears in the eyes can see rainbows

Live in the moment

I have never met a strong person with an easy past

Idea pitch

"Italians have a little joke that the world is so hard a man must have two fathers to look after him, and that's why they have godfathers."
— *The Godfather*

Dream run interrupted by wakeup call

Its alcohol fuelled wisdom

Reduced to a foot note

In real world scenario

Given the short time line I am looking for quick turn around

Positive illusions

In intended consequences

Give thy thoughts no tongue

Glorious past but penurious present

Highest ethical behavior is competitive advantage

People or situation is powerless without your reaction

Fragile coexistence

He was a dreamer, a thinker, a speculative philosopher... or, as his wife would have it, an idiot.

Pulling weight more than its strength

Heart at the right place

Changing optics

Hitting all the wrong notes

A memorial to immortalize shame

Muscular talk

Compelling explanation

God when I lose hope help me to remember that your love is greater than my disappointments and your plans for my life are better than my dreams

---

Reverse transition

Life is short smile till you have teeth

But, except for a brief period after independence when the idea of an inclusive India - a haven for liberal and plural values and a democracy built on the rights and obligations of citizenship, thrived and seemed to take root - it has mostly been a relentless slide towards what may become a tragic parody of what we wanted to become as a nation and society

---

Time is an illusion, lunch time is doubly so

Send to the men who need a laugh and the women with a good sense of humor

---

Hitting all the wrong notes

A memorial to immortalize shame

Best fights are the ones we avoid

Muscular talk

If you think only with your eyes so you are easy to fool

Compelling explanation

Here are the two rules of Karate….
Rule one Karate is for defense only
Rule two learn the rule number one

Offer your whole self

Low end generic strategy

Lift and shift strategy

Well founded need

This is toughest indicator to excel with

A little girl in every one of us comes out

Non refulgent

Upping the program

Building transition response programs

Always listen to reason

One must be vigilant not to lose one's temper on trivial and petty matters, for that will retard his progress. Anger must be sublimated by systematic effort. One must resist the impulse to enter into discussions and arguments, for this breeds a spirit of rivalry and leads one towards feelings of anger and vengeance. Anger is at the root of all wrong behavior. Hence, cultivate love towards all beings and thus keep undesirable habits and tendencies at bay

---

Prepare you for road and not prepare road for you

Profit appetite

At fifty everyone has the face he deserves.
    - George Orwell

Critical mass

All photos are accurate because none of them is the truth

Karmic baggage

Overlord

All weather friend - fair weather friend

Law of Equal Opportunity

1. You cannot legislate the poor into prosperity by legislating the wealthy out of prosperity
2. What one person receives without working for, another person must work for without receiving
3. The government cannot give to anybody anything that the government does not first take from somebody else

---

You cannot multiply wealth by dividing it!

When half of the people get the idea that they do not have to work

Because the other half is going to take care of them,

And when the other half gets the idea that it does no good to work because somebody else is going to get what they work for, that is the beginning of the end of any nation.

Applying his own medicine

Showing spine

Burnt his way into development

It is in the cross hairs

There is a theory which states that if ever anyone discovers exactly what the Universe is for and why it is here, it will instantly disappear and be replaced by something even more bizarre and inexplicable. There is another theory which states that this has already happened

--Douglas Adams

Dubious blessing

Every morning ask
What are the 3 things we do differently today?

Massive wave of entrepreneurial energy coursing through Indian arteries

---

Stretched the melodic horizon

In the circles in which we move it is easy to come across clever men but difficult to find virtuous ones

---

Innovate or you are toast

Sword of revolution is sharpened on whetting stone of ideas

We waste time looking for the perfect lover, instead of creating the perfect love

---

There is nothing as useless as doing efficiently that which should not be done at all

---

I like deadlines; I like the whooshing sound they make as they fly by
  - Douglas Adams

Until the lion learns to write its own, every story will always try to glorify the hunter

---

That is the greatness of Gandhi, whose birth anniversary we have just celebrated. Through all our failings and infirmities he put the humblest among us in touch with what is most noble in our collective consciousness

---

Ferocious sense of entitlement

If slaughter houses have glass walls everyone would have been vegetarian

---

I am not afraid of an army of lions led by a sheep but I am afraid of an army of sheep led by lion
– Alexander

When they die, part of me will die

The regal city of Hyderabad is choc-o-bloc with activities and places enough for you to be spoilt for choices

---

Your focus needs more focus

Rattling the chess board of Indian polity

Rolling back frontiers of state in financial controls

Incrementalism than big bang

Injecting greater efficiency into a flawed system

Float like a butterfly sting like a bee

The effort of US is to midwife the unity of two countries

We gain the strength of the temptation we resist

Explanation of anger; not expression of anger

It is not the mountains ahead to climb that wear you out but the pebble in your shoe
   – Md Ali

Globe circling cyber phenomenon

Dark and brooding genius

Muzzling the dissent

What is left now of the idea of India?

The expansive cultural sensibility, the persistent sense of wonder and curiosity, the delight in open discourse and debate with no point of view discarded, and above all the embrace of humanity with all its quirks and eccentricities - these have been the hallmark of a civilization which has mostly seen itself as a journey not a destination.

Its innate mental construct has refused to divide humanity into the sterile categories of We and They. Departures from this template have mercifully been brief - even if, on occasion, violent and destructive. There have always been, through our tumultuous history, wise and sagacious Indians who have reminded us of the virtues of tolerance and sharing, of compassion and humanity, which is the unique legacy of this land.

Our land is the repository of the most sublime music, the most incredible sculpture, the most profound literature in a variety of languages and a highly developed and subtle understanding of aesthetics

Successful management of the multiplicities which rapid technological change is forcing humanity to confront

---

The Indian spirit in its most refined articulations has been an outstanding example of a comfortable coexistence and sharing of diverse cultures and traditions, ways of thinking and living. But we are in danger of losing our USP even though much of the world still comes to our shores to seek the wisdom which could restore humanity amidst a rising tide of extremism, cruelty and barbaric violence

---

Connecting to second meal

Be a ladder and not leader

Intellectual muddle

Half way civilized society

Unless each one is respected, whatever his status, his economic condition, his Spiritual development, there can be no peace and no happiness in life. This respect can be aroused only by the conviction that the same Soul that is in you, is playing the role of the other person. See that Soul in others; feel that they too have hunger, thirst, yearning and distress you have; develop sympathy and the anxiety to serve and be useful.

Tax terrorism

Low lying fruit

Acrimonious exchanges

The street reactions for the incident would not have been couched in niceties

---

Their reactions are unwaveringly hostile

International "rent a cause brigade"

Quasi Fuehrer

Language is joint creation of poets and manual workers

Pulse of life depends on blood of others

Enabling foot hold in the economic ladder

We come together only to go apart again. The law of life can't be avoided. The law comes into operation the moment we detach ourselves from our mother's womb. All struggle & misery in life is due to our attempt to arrest this law or get away from it or in allowing ourselves to be hurt by it. The fact must be recognized. A profound unmitigated loneliness is the only truth of life. All else is false. The law of life - No sense in battling against it..."

- R.K. Narayan

Mistakes fed on each other

Textual than contextual

Recall value

For every credibility gap there is gullibility filling

Indian politician gets money from rich and votes from poor; protect them from each other

---

Micro enterprise is not relative of micro finance, it is its twin

---

We must learn to honor excellence in every socially accepted human activity, however humble the activity, and to scorn shoddiness, however exalted the activity. An excellent plumber is infinitely more admirable than an incompetent philosopher. The society that scorns excellence in plumbing because plumbing is a humble activity and tolerates shoddiness in philosophy because it is an exalted activity will have neither good plumbing nor good philosophy. Neither its pipes nor its theories will hold water.

-John W. Gardner

Nature is what we are put in this world rise above

If there is to be any peace, it will come through being, not having

---

Hereditary asses

Being still and doing nothing are two very different things.

Rule of law and rule of life

The human DNA is imprinted with a natural propensity to favor own community

---

Caught in wrong instincts

Re optimizing the strategies

How our plans hinge on interactions with existing interventions

---

Where you live should not decide whether you live

What they repay is tears

Understandable challenges

Potentially condemning millions to remain in poverty

To die rich is dying in disgrace
-Melinda Gates

If you succeed lead otherwise guide

Respect yourself enough to walk away from anything that no longer serves you, grows you or makes you happy

---

Life is 10% what happens to you and 90% how you respond

Pyramid came crashing

Turning program inputs into outcomes

They shall mount up with wings as eagles
They shall run and not wary

You are what you eat

Blood sucking shylocks

In the twilight zone

Claw its way back

Nothing exists for itself alone
But only in relation to other forms of life

Pakistanis think that Islam is born in 1947

Navigating the organization through challenging times

Finding the lowest hanging fruit

Limited command over resources

Loaded with bribes

Management is doing things right, leadership is doing right things

---

Leadership is made of results not attributes

Market based procedure

Disproportionately affects the poorest most vulnerable women

Knockout test

Freedom is not worth having if it does not include the freedom to mistake

---

Cycle of gloom and doom

You can make more friends in two months by being interested in other people than in two years of trying to get people interested in you
— Dale Carnegie

It is bureaucracy that pushes poverty to borders and worse when there is no debate

---

Avoid the acute angle

And when all the wars are over a butterfly will still be beautiful
- Ruskin Bond

Mr. Fix it

Risk appetite

Sequencing the support

Exception proves the rule

Caught in the cross hairs

Context matters

Love is the answer, but while you're waiting for the answer, sex raises some pretty good questions
  – WOODY ALLEN

I may not be there
Yet closer than yesterday

Additive impacts

Fat hopes

Lowest quintile of the poorest

Loan default turned into uncontrolled epidemic

Opening can of worms

We train our characters to be passive

What you will be is what you do now
  - The Buddha

Power is terrifying
But more terrifying in the hands of its abuser

Opportunities in the organization are limited only to the imagination of your mind

---

World has no option but to bow down to your strength

Mindfully engaged

Leading edge solution

Women under the yoke of religion

In the beginning there was no center
In the beginning there was not margin
Then what existed before margin and center?
    - Rig Veda

Cynic knows price of everything and value of nothing

Regrets are the natural property of grey hairs

Emotional boundaries

Attempting to widen the latitude

Over scrupulous in the arrangement of her attire

Challenge the prevailing assumptions with a single question; why and put the same question relentlessly to those responsible for the current way of doing things until they are sick of it

---

Symbiotic universe

Break loose; free yourself from dysfunctional people

Who are experts at meeting their own needs at the expense of yours

Don't let people stay in your life who trample on your feelings and behave badly

Set clean boundaries so that you don't get caught up their maze of madness or feel responsible for their life choices or consequences

Live your own story

Don't try to edit someone else's

Practice radical self care and work to maintain your peace of mind

Do something every day that nourishes your spirit, opens heart and builds mutual resiliency, it's your life, live intentionally with purpose and passion

---

Who are you to decide for us?

"I have loved the stars too fondly to be fearful of the night."
~ Galileo

Entry barriers

To be without some of the things you want is an indispensable part of happiness

---

Marginal mountain economy

Degree of one's emotions is inversely proportional to the one's knowledge of facts

---

Happy family is earlier heaven
Unhappy one is earlier hell

God overestimated his ability while creating man

"Most people trusted in the future, assuming that their preferred version of it would unfold, blindly planning for it, and envisioning things that weren't the case. This was the working of the will. This was what gave the

world purpose and direction. Not what was there but what was not."
— Jhumpa Lahiri

Heart that never hardens

Temper that never tires

Touch that never hurts

Herd instinct out of collective fear against non-members of the herd

---

We only forge the chains that we wear in life

They deserve less judgment, more understanding and better support

---

Non-agricultural competencies

Some vices are virtues carried to excess, they are not really vices

---

War does not determine who is right - only who is left
- Bertrand Russell

Marginal productivity hooks them to agriculture but not bring out of poverty

---

Agricultural poverty trap

There are also people at the right side of the spectrum

Tunisia is a democratic beacon in a vast swathe between Iran to Morocco

---

My father named me....
He did not make me ......

It is part of larger destiny

An hour of basketball feels like 15 minutes. An hour on a treadmill feels like a weekend in driving school
  – DAVID WALTERS

Pathologically lying

India is slipping into China's shadow

We who lived in concentration camps can remember the men who walked through the huts comforting others, giving away their last piece of bread. They may have been few in number, but they offer sufficient proof that everything can be taken from a man but one thing: the last of the human

freedoms, to choose one's attitude in any given set of circumstances."
   --Victor Frankl

If wealth was inevitable result of hard work and enterprise, every rural woman should have been a millionaire

---

I survived another meeting that should have been an e-mail

Finite disappointment is defeated by infinite hope

People can always be brought to the biddings of their leaders

---

Pious generalities

Verbal offences

Half brained

Humor impaired

Courtesy is two way traffic

I would rather die on my two feet than live on my knees

He is caught in the pincer of a paradox

Predicament of Indian intellectual in the high noon of Nehruvian era

---

Insolent disregard for social mores

Too close to America; too far from God
   - A Mexican saying

Confident walk vs. confused run

If you can count your money then go back to work

He who is only just is cruel. Who on earth could live were all judged justly?

Rolling back state Incrementalism than big bang, injecting greater efficiency into a flawed system

---

One good thing about Stones – they come in our way as hurdles, but once we pass them, they automatically become our mile stones

---

When you have more than you need, build longer table, not higher fence

---

The way to a man's heart is through his stomach

America did not invent human rights; in true sense human rights invented America
   - Jimmy Carter

Never be too proud

Never be too bossy

Remember that you live in a planet that has gravity

What goes up must come down

Humility counts

Aspiring for decent piece of global pie

Seeing through the Anti India vitriol in text books

The whole warmth is subdued by meta narratives

The line between good and evil is permeable and anyone can be induced to cross it pressured by situational force

---

Majoritarian inevitability

Words are a mirror of their times. By looking at the areas in which the vocabulary of a language is expanding fastest in a given period, we can form a fairly accurate impression of the chief preoccupations of society at that time and the points at which the boundaries of human Endeavour are being advanced.
  -John Ayto

I am not interested whether you have sat with the greats, but definitely on whether you have sat with the broken

---

Jumped out of corporate cubicle

Ears that do not listen to advice, accompany the head when it is chopped off

~African Proverb

Do not speak badly of yourself, for the warrior within hears your words and lessened by them

---

May my heart be kind, my mind fierce and spirit brave

Never hate your enemies, it affects your judgment

US is retooling its Afghan approach

They have bone to pick up

Every pen makes its own tune so is everyone's gun

If you work for a living, why do you kill yourself working?

The best way to predict future is to create it
- Peter Drucker

Originality is the art of concealing your source

The customer now has the information.... the manufacturer will cease to be a seller and instead become a buyer for the customer; new mantra of online shopping

---

Great literature is simply language charged with meaning to the utmost possible degree

---

He got an excuse of his height to make it to the Chess team

First I was dying to finish high school and join college. And then I was dying to finish college and start working. And then I was dying to marry and have children. And then I was dying for my children to grow old enough for school so I could return to work. And then I was dying to retire. And now I am dying …And suddenly I realize I forgot to live

---

You can catch more flies with honey than with vinegar

Age is not important unless you are a cheese

We have probed the earth, excavated it, burned it, ripped things from it, buried things in it, chopped down its forests, leveled its hills, muddied its waters, and dirtied its air. That does not fit my definition of a good tenant. If we were here on a month-to-month basis, we would have been evicted long ago.
    - Rose Bird, Chief Justice of California Supreme Court

I never learned from a man who agrees with me

Anyone who considers protocol unimportant, has never dealt with a cat

---

If you even dream of beating me you'd better wake up and apologize.
    - Muhammad Ali

I am destroyed but not defeated

Her dress was so annoying I cursed that all her kids will be born completely naked

---

She is cocooning herself and not coming out

You are poor if you have too much month at the end of money

Happiness can exist only in acceptance

Giving an appearance of solidity to wind

Freedom is the right to tell people what they do not want to hear
    - George Orwell

A mass of lies

Politicians should always be judged guilty until they are proved innocent

---

Truly competing sport is nothing but war minus shooting

All efforts of the country have not brought the equality a millimeter nearer

---

Emotional sincerity

Thought police

As couple if you can live through the remodeling of the house, you can live rest of the lives together

---

Politicians are like sperm, one in million turns out to be human being

---

People will never forget how you made them feel

Tending our inner gardens

He imagines his intelligence to be sieve of closely woven mesh through which nothing but the finest can pass

---

No one has invented a condom for the pen yet

In Delhi death and drink make life worth living

Readers are the invisible listeners with whom the writer strikes a sympathetic chord

---

I allowed my memory to journey back to the days of my childhood

---

The part of India I love and live does not make head lines

Treasure Love for your family, love for your spouse and love for your friends
Treat yourself well. Cherish others.

Biting wit

It forms dark counter point to our national culture

Every word has consequences. Every silence too

If plan A doesn't work, there are 25 more letters in the alphabets

---

His writings are stinging slap to establishment

Laying of the fact checkers

The unthinkable is now more possible than it has ever been

Poverty is when you have too much month at the end of your money

---

Bending backwards

Life journey to a place where there was nowhere left to go

She has the gift of accepting her life
   - Jumpa Lahiri

Achiever is like a pressure cooker with certain amount of pressure already in it. The more you let out the less you cook

---

Simple is harder than the complex

The blanket of my fate is woven black
Even the best river cannot wash it white

She is a kite dancing in hurricane

The ideological fervor is not so intense with its sympathizers

---

The very bastion of secularism has come under squeeze

War is continuation of politics by other means

Focusing only on Resume is like saving sex for old age

Fixing the leaky pipes

"One reason why birds and horses are not unhappy is because they are not trying to impress other birds and horses."
— Dale Carnegie

It's me, the author of all your pain
— Villain's dialogue in a cinema

Orchestrated hysteria

They conspired an epic crime against humanity

It is a policy that satisfies the definition of genocide

He is consumed by regret and contrition

Feeding the journalists with factoids of sanitized intelligence

---

Informed memory

Transparent lies

Lethal hypocrisy

Like Ebola from West Africa a bacteria called perpetual war has crossed the Atlantic

---

Sociopathic verboseness

The issue is the most festering open wound

Powerless people will find powerless means of response when they are attacked

---

One of the truest tests of integrity is its blunt refusal to be compromised

---

Fasten your seat belts it is going to be bumpy night!!!

People come into our lives for a reason

Wrongs will be righted if we are united

Music is the shorthand of emotion

You don't have to live life by the Book.
Make your own story

I am the rest between two notes which are somehow always discord

---

Mobilizing consensus vs. molding consensus

Person in a set of circumstances
And a person with certain set of attitudes

Living in pitiless times of war and conflict

We are but what we repeatedly do;
Excellence then is not an act but habit

If you can't see yourself doing anything else and you have the drive and ambition, get the training and go for it

---

He looked at me the way all the women wanted to be looked at by a man

---

Art is the only way to runaway without leaving home
   - Twyla Tharp

A snake starts to rattle because he is scared
  - Unknown author

Courage cannot erase fears; courage is when we face our fears

---

Politics is the easiest to play in the beginning and hardest to master at the end

---

To be nice is different than to be good and to be good is different than to be right

---

The one thing that you have that nobody has is you. Your voice your mind your story and your vision. So write and draw and build and play and dance and live only as you can

---

Too many years fighting back the tears, why can't the past just die?

My eyes always water at this part
  - Quantum of Opera

It's a sick joke

There are advantages to being President. The day after I was elected, I had my High school grades classified Top Secret
   – RONALD REAGAN

The opposite of war is not peace; it is creation

My heart is like sea, a million dreams are in it

Impossible things are happening everyday

You are never fully dressed without a smile

The music is not in the notes but in the silence between

Climb every mountain, ford every stream and follow every rainbow till you find your dream

---

Cherry picked sob stories of the media

Massive forced suicide of Europe with immigration crisis

May be we can't be okay;
But may we are tough
And we will try anyway

What does not kill us makes us hotter

They say for every light in Broadway there is a broken heart, an unrealized dream. And that is the same in any profession. So you have to want it more than anyone else and you have to be your own champion, be your own super star, blaze your own path, say yes to opportunity, follow your instincts, be eager and passionate and keep learning. Nurture your real lasting relationships. Don't be a jerk and free your imagination so you will become all that you want to be.
   - Sutton Foster

I don't cause commotions, I am one

The futility of revolutionaries who have no gardens, who depend on the very system they attack and who produce words and bullets and not food and shelter

---

We as species have choice to continue to develop our bodies and brains in a healthy upward trajectory

---

I grew up learning to hide my caste as I was backward

He wanted to become a Karl Sagan
But Karl Marx ruined him

Actors without stage hands are naked people in the dark trying to emote

Stage hands without actors are at the bar

When you are married you will understand the importance of fresh produce

---

The belt was his favorite child development tool
   - An unknown about his father

Money, if you pardon the expression, is like manure. It's not worth a thing unless its spreads around encouraging young things to grow
   - Dialogue in Hello Dolly

Theatre is the only institution that has been dying for 4000 years and has never succumbed

---

The only thing better than singing is more singing

I regard theatre as the greatest of all art forms. The most immediate way in which a human being can share with another the sense of what it is to be human being
   - Oscar Wilde

All I wanted was to be loved for myself

It is a world where everything breaks down into song and dance

---

I have got a lot of living to do

I am confused by life and I feel safe within the confines of theatre

---

There is that smaller world which is the stage and the larger stage which is the world

---

The past can hurt either we run from it or learn from it

What makes us special and what makes us strong are not different

---

Opportunity is not a lengthy visitor

Restores the idea of India to its due dignity, an idea wounded seriously over the last few years

---

Stay humble, grounded and focused

The man who knows his cow wins; the one who pretends to love it loses in at the end

---

India investment ease rating has fallen to neutral from most overweight

---

Adapt themes rooted in social values

If you hire only those people you understand, the company will never get people better than you are. Always remember that you often find outstanding people among those you don't particularly like
  - Soichiro Honda

Non-reciprocal magnanimity

Their policy suffers from an empathy deficit and is characterized by disregard for the sensibilities of the neighbor countries

---

Progress is man's ability to complicate simplicity

I am lover not fighter
But I can fight to defend my love

The art of relationship is like musical instrument; first you must learn to play by rules, then you forget rules and play from the heart

---

The best thing one can do when it's raining is to let it

There is a saying: yesterday is history, tomorrow is a mystery, but today is a gift.

That is why it is called the present

Tweaking the facial nerves

Your skills are now at the point of spiritual insight

They worshipped strength, because it is strength that makes all other values possible. Nothing survives without it. Who knows what delicate wonders have died out of the world, for want of the strength to survive?

No matter how beautiful and handsome you are just remember baboon and gorillas also attract tourists

– stop boasting

No matter how big and strong you are you will not carry yourself to your grave

– be humble

No matter how tall you are you can never see tomorrow

– be patient

No matter how light skinned you are you will always need light in darkness

– take caution

No matter how rich and many cars you have you always walk into your house
   - Be grounded

Journey of life ...

We pass pleasures and pains

There will be sunshine and rain

There will be loss and gain

But must we learn to

Smile again and again

Life will knock us down, but we can choose whether or not to stand back up

---

Our patriotic ideology is so much enmeshed with our religious theology

---

We are unlikely to achieve a "light bulb" moment of epiphany with a neatly presented answer for this question.

FDI in India is one way street, the investors take much more than what they bring in

---

To forgive terrorists is up to God

But to send them to Him is up to me
   - Putin

My head aches with silent rage
I fear myself, a feeling strange
A numbing of senses, a transition stage
Where will he take me his violent sage

By becoming interested in the cause we are less likely
to dislike the effect

One cannot hire a hand; the whole man always comes
with it
   - Peter Drucker

Monotony reveals our limitations

When flood comes, fish eats ants and when flood
recedes, ants eat fish
Only time matters. Just hold on. Nature gives
opportunity to everyone.

In a theatre when drama plays, you opt for front seats.
When film is screened, you opt for rear seats. Your
position in life is only relative. Not absolute.

For making soap, oil is required. But to clean oil, soap
is required. This is the irony of life

Every problem has (N+1) solutions: where N is the number of solutions that you have tried and 1 is that you have not tried.

Only two types of people are happy in life - the Mad and the Child. Be Mad to achieve a goal. Be a Child to enjoy what you achieved.

Euphoric tone unmarred by any whiff from piles of corpses

When you run it's called race, and when god runs with you it's called Grace

---

A rare instance where an element of architectural embellishment has caught the imagination of the masses ensuring instant recognition for all those associated with the monument

---

Mathematics may not teach us how to add happiness or how to minus sadness

But it does teach one important thing every problem has a solution

---

Not responding is a response

Cherry picking the events from history

Words are pegs to hang ideas on

The future's got a million roads for you to choose,
But you will walk a little taller in some high heel shoes
   - Hairspray

A jellyfish swam in a tropical sea
And he said, "This world just consists of me"
There is nothing above or nothing below
That a jellyfish ever can properly know.
"So I come at last to the plain conclusion,
Which is fairly set free from any confusion,
That the Universe simply centers in me
And if I were not, then nothing would be."
That moment a shark who was strolling by
Just gulped him down in the blink of an eye.
And he died with a few convulsive twists
But somehow the Universe still exists.
   - Grant Allen

Talk only if you can improve upon silence

Inch of action is better than miles of intention

Belied expectations

Alcohol is for people who can afford to lose some brain cells

---

We haven't yet learned how to stay human when assembled in masses.
- Lewis Thomas

When the power of love overcomes the love of power the world will know peace

---

The optics re affirmed that he is the real boss

Journey from ration card to credit card

Salary comes at 2 G speed and goes at 4 G speed

I am because we are
- A team building theme

He started staking claim on global game of chickens

Here your own voices in the backwaters of silence

Speak softly but carry big stick

Media is drawn into the political vortex

'Arms length' approach

Gratitude is like electricity it should be produced, discharged and used to exist well

---

Calibrated strategy

An old miser kept a tame jackdaw that used to steal pieces of money, and hide them in a hole, which a cat observing, asked, "Why he would hoard up those round shining things that he could make no use of?" "Why," said the jackdaw, "my master has a whole chestful, and makes no more use of them than I do."
   - Jonathan Swift

The country was brought to its knees by terrorist actions

Irrevalance of peaceful majority

Intermittency of non-conventional energy makes it technically unviable

---

Climate change resulted in extreme weather but our development resulted in chaos

---

The chinks in defense of the country

Incubating the innovations

Fame is a bee

It has a song

It has a sting

Ah, too, it has a wing

The party is yet to get its acts together
    - Jimi Hendrix

The irrepressible trouble maker

Meteorological oddity of the region

Be CEO of your life

He blurted his inner contempt for the country

A strong marriage is not about 2 strong persons at the same time. It's the partners who take turns to being strong for each other in the moments the other partner is week

---

I am because we are

All words are pegs to hang on ideas in mind

Ideological fervor is not so intense with the sympathizer

Bastion of secularism came under seize

Gave a stinging slap

Sin Tax

As far as I am concerned the scariest thing to come from Muslim community is Algebra

---

He is pleasantly disarming, affable and polite off the court as he is aggressive on it

---

I am good loser

Feel like the only one in universe

Be who you needed when you are youngest

The thing you fight you become the one

People with verbal diarrhea

Skill is muscle of livelihoods

Profit is identified with money but real profit is dignity and satisfaction

---

Co-creating prosperity

I am reinventing myself

Your intellect is teenier and tinier than your brain

Large no., of services and interventions should be bundled together to straddle value chain

---

Policy is following than leading

Unlocking the value chain

The strength of the chain is "its weakest link"

Climate resilient

Handle every stressful situation like a dog if you can't eat or play with it just pee it and walk away

---

I am the worst thing that ever happened

Carnival barker

Outcomes rarely turn on grand gestures or the art of the deal,

But on whether you've sent someone a thank-you note
  – BERNIE

Increasingly bigoted shoot from the hip

Style is time's fool; form is time's student

Incendiary call

He had grand illusion of adequacy

Provider's land scape of skilling

To resonate this point

When all their programs failed, they blamed the poor for being poor

---

A leader is a dealer in hope

Its farcical proposition and cruel joke

We have trust surplus but capital deficit

Corporates owe a collective apology

It is structural impossibility

Patronizing - give a man a fish and he can eat for a day. Give him a fishing rod and he can feed himself. Alternatively don't poison the fishing waters

Abduct his great grandparents into slavery then turn up 400 years later on your gap year talking a lot of shit about fish

---

The issue is hitting a nerve

A leg up the ladder

Colonialism is one of those things you are not supposed to discuss in polite company at least not the north of the Mediterranean most

---

Wise men find more opportunities than they get

Lies and Plastic smiles

Rear guard battle

The soul should always stand ajar; ready to welcome the ecstatic experience
   - Emily Dickinson

Chink in defense

There is no market for your emotions; never advertise your feelings; show only just your attitude

---

Pathological consumption

Critics seem to have wrong maths on this issue

'Great' is the guilt of unnecessary war

Moral panic

Global shaper

Man is free at the moment he wishes to be

The area is powder keg with serious animosities between two communities

---

It's about how the concept is rewiring the tribal mind

Help the people grind a new set of glasses so that they can see the world in a new way

---

Fiscal space

Republicans are so bullish that 30% of them would vote for bombing fictional country

---

Mobile has brought us three things
Whatever makes you happy save
Whatever makes others happy forward
Whatever will make no one happy delete?

Nothing in life comes easy
Even Santa comes with a clause

Wear your failure as badge of honor

Collateral reasons

Bold choices and mistakes are all those things that add up to the person you become

---

The party closed ranks behind the person

It is yet to get its acts together

Traffic logjam, it is the only time I get to be myself

People call me a feminist whenever I express sentiments that differentiate me from a doormat.
    - Rebecca West

The only thing that comes to us without effort is old age

Problems are only opportunities in work clothes

Smart is knowing the difference between motion and direction

Very often change of self is needed than change of scene

Drowning in information
But starving for knowledge

Two ways of living – as though everything is miracle and the other as though nothing is miracle

---

Like a coin time can be spent in any side, but only once

Team work divides the effort; multiplies the effect

Every blade of grass has an angel that bends over it
And whispers 'grow, grow'

Externalizing costs is integral to profits

When exponential technology is 1% you are half way
to 100%

A good conscience is continual Christmas

If I got my zeroes right

Men build too many walls and not enough bridges

We are all now connected by the internet like neurons
in a giant brain

Words are a commodity in which there is no slump

Enterprise through Symbiotic Market Models

Social responsibility and commercialization are
mutually reinforcing verticals

Let us move from market economy to market society where markets and market values completely penetrate spheres of life traditionally governed by non-market norms

- Michel Sandel

About Social Enterprise

Social responsibility is moral limit of markets. It is surplus generating but also social maximizing. It is having business competency with social passion and true inclusion. It may be optimal or suboptimal yet sustainable in its result. Its stake holding is about thresholds and not maximization.

Symbiotic markets are internally focused with surpluses appropriately entering external markets – not the reverse. Social sector and stake can co-exist – you have to simply redraw the boundaries Enterprise stake is in width, depth and length; depth being social responsibility. It needs Analytical separation of profit and social responsibility and not as mutual exclusivity.

My long innings in professional development work is rooted in evidence based social enterprise models

---

Pursuing the idea to move from the classical charity mode to doing responsible profitable business with far and wide reaching impact on the disadvantaged constituencies we wish to serve

---

He renewed his pitch for free internet

Strong gate keeper

A depressing goal

How did it get so late so soon?

You have to be a stupid to hang on to your idea

Polar melt

Are you not in the swim?

To be dissolved into something complete

God has crumbled up the old moon into stars

Holding the universe together

Sometimes I can feel my bones straining under the weight of all the lives I'm not living."

Let me something every minute of my life

The curves of your lips rewrite history
    - Oscar Wilde

Whatever our souls are made of; his and mine are the same

If equal affection cannot be, let the more loving one be me.

Now that you don't have to be perfect, you can be good

In that particular moment we were infinite

What Am I up to?

My endeavor is embedded in social enterprise that hinges on multi optimization on dimensions of people, planet and profits. It is meant to transform poverty to sustainability and charity to opportunity by steering economically active but resource poor, creating pathways out of poverty. It sequences existing safety net programs with opportunity new livelihoods. Its mind is in EROI (economic return on investment) but heart in SROI (social return on investment) This echoes the outcry of our rural and tribal poor, **'we want opportunity not charity, let our products reach your markets'.**

Focus is to create fragrance and use wind:

I. The Fragrance: providing affordable solutions and create show case models

II. **The wind**: Measuring evidence and disseminating for upscale benefits

---

Slogan:

'More with less'

We have tested waters but we wanted to sail across We wanted to come out of resource limited circumstances but not to be lost into cash flow chasing **return on capital** instead **return of capital**. At present we are working in unfair constraints addressing multitude of vulnerabilities in social enterprise space. We are restless optimists. We have broken margins and instead of flying with mind in corporate space we have stayed back with heart in social enterprise arena.

Model:

The scale intensity is going to be high through global dissemination and show casing the model that can be emulated by likeminded budding social entrepreneurs. It is demonstrable impact setting new bench mark globally. It is basically to pull appropriate models from black holes of its technologies and enterprise. It is dynamic mosaic resting on a new paradigm allowing us to use our rich enterprise experience, what we fondly call community owned 4C approach – cultivation, consumption, conservation and commerce

Impact:

We expect our work to be evaluated by distance travelled and not its peak of excellence.

The Social Business Opportunity

We found social business opportunity by making user friendly marketing models pulling down elite curtains built by technocrat companies to inflate costs. Real stake in enterprise is in engaging and including communities into value chains and markets in a sustainable and equitable way. The challenge is in creating "symbiotic market model". The revenue model is 'user groups are dealer groups".

Enterprise is application of innovations to responsibly leverage base of pyramid opportunities in emerging markets not about high voltage profits alone.

It might be that to surrender to happiness was to accept defeat, but it was a defeat better than many victories

---

There is a sense in which we are all each other's consequences

---

At the still point there the dance is
    - TS Eliot

Her laughter was a question he wanted to spend his whole life answering

---

The pieces I am, she gathered them and gave them back to me in all the right order

---

He is nearer to the wild heart of life

She was lost in her longing to understand

She was becoming herself, casting aside that fictitious self like, a garment with which to appear before the world

---

We cross our bridges as we come to them and burn them behind us, with nothing to show for our progress except a memory of the smell of smoke and the presumption that once our eyes watered."

The half life of love is forever

Tomorrow is always fresh with no mistakes in it yet

I would always rather be happy than dignified

Tread softly because you are treading on my dreams

It frightened him to think what must have gone to the making of her eyes

---

It does not do well to dwell on dreams and forget to live
    —J.K. Rowling

I am full of mistakes and imperfections and therefore I am real

---

Egregious nepotism

To clear the Augean stables

Flying re-imagined

What screws us up most in life is the picture in our head of how it's supposed to be

---

We may live under the same sky but not in the same horizons

Humor is the reason gone mad

Create templates for the steps forward

Anonymous Soldiers quipping

Either I will come back after hoisting the tricolor or I will come back wrapped in it but I will be back for sure

---

What is life time adventure to you is daily routine to us

To find us you must be good, to catch us you must be fast but to beat us you must be kidding

---

May God have mercy on our enemies because we don't have

If a man says he is not afraid of dying he is either kidding or he is a Gorkha

---

It is the God's duty to forgive the enemies but it is our duty to convene a meeting between the two

---

Way to catalyze solutions for jig saw puzzle

The only way out is through

Doom that is due

Tele reported to adventures

Don't live the same year 75 times and call it life

A point of view can be dangerous luxury when substituted for in sight and understanding

---

Sent backwards all his life to win support of people

Destiny is not shoes we wear but steps we take

Camping – Nature's way of promoting motel industry

We have to let go off the life we have planned so as to have the life waiting for us.

Our work is only as meaningful as the lives we transform

Rich possibilities

Running through the tunnel

Oxy moron

Courage is grace under pressure

Horses for courses

Ready to hit the road

Playing hard ball

It's not miles honey, it is mileage
- Dialogue in a holly wood cinema

Let us not pray to be sheltered from dangers but to be fearless when facing them
- Rabindra Nath Tagore

See through the game

Fathers who are too liberal or too repressive are not fathers; they are either step fathers or friends

---

It has communal spin

Humor is reason gone mad
  - Grucho Marx

You can't out run your fate

Only dead fish go with flow

There is no lock without key and no problem without solution

Skewed priorities

The hope of a secure and livable world lies with non conformists

Who are dedicated to justice, peace and brotherhood. The trailblazers in human, academic, scientific and religious freedom have always been non conformists. In any cause that concerns the progress of mankind put your faith in the non conformists
  - Martin Luther King

You have to be a stupid to hang on to your idea

Intense downward pressure on wages of unskilled and less skilled laborers

---

It epitomizes the conservative model

Boom and bust cycles of emerging markets

The yield of the system is theoretically unlimited

Everything gardens itself

Less about slipping into glass slippers and more about shattering glass ceilings

---

Pyramid to Diamond structure

Super market catchment

Co-creation of value

Going to hit us slam bang

Risk aversion of farmers

If sex ratio of the country is 999 to 1000 male, I remained the one without partner

---

I am team Roger Fetherer

A straight line even in ECG means we are not live; so is life without struggles

---

Chiseled prose

The grass may be greener on the other side, but it is as hard to cut

---

Treacherous hypocrisies

Refuse to allow illness a place in your consciousness

Laugh riot with fun side up

If triangles had God he would have been 3 sided

There is more to boxing than hitting, not getting hit, for instance

---

Just because some people are fueled by drama doesn't mean you have to attend the performance

---

The idea lays bare the hypocrisies of the society

Unbroken history of broken promises

Scorching pace

Entrepreneurial explosion

Success is ability to go from one failure to another
failure without loss of enthusiasm
   - Churchill

Secret sauce

Breaking ranks with

You may bend the truth but can't break it

I take full responsibility for letting you use me

Organic farms will turn you into tree when you die

Before you judge me walk in my shoes, live my sorrow,
my doubts, my fear, my pain and my laughter

Ancient prejudice and modern inequality

The incident lays bare the tragic in equality undergirding the modern state and its institutions

---

Archaic arithmetic of politics

Our lives to begin to end the day we become silent about things that matter

---

Before you release words shape them with no sharp edges so they don't hurt anyone they hit

---

For marriage to be success every woman and every man should have her and his own bathrooms

---

May God restore you to the fullness and purpose He designed for you

---

Arc of moral universe is long but it bends to justice

People normally want to see you doing better but not better than them

---

Fringe candidate

Between the informed and the imagined

Falling head over heels for literature

Grand standing

The richer the one percent gets the worse of everyone else

Build firm foundations with the bricks others have thrown at you

---

Never approach a bull from front, a horse from back and an idiot from any side

---

Those who dream in the day are cognizant of many things which escape those who dream only nights

---

The public is merely a multiplied 'me'
  - Mark Twain

Side by side or miles apart
But always connected by heart

The Gods of the valley are not the Gods of the hills

It is bad news that our nationalism has to be certified by extreme rightists, it is the worst news that the state sanctions those of us who do not get certified.

Slogan on demand for timely wages
"Pay the laborer before his sweat dries"

Growing old is compulsory "growing up" is optional

Light does not get dimmer with the string of Sun

Mad respect

Who you think you cannot continue to live without …..

One generation back people were born in their grandparents houses so they visited their grandparent's house frequently, now people are born in hospitals so they visit hospitals frequently

---

The company is making killing out of plummeting crude prices

By launch of his product he plans to unleash a big disruption in the sector

---

I have never met a strong person with an easy past

Be in touch with yourself

Tax allergic business regimen

"Whistle to dog" arrangement

The company has young blood streaming in its veins

Keep being you, don't let someone else's bitterness change the person you are

---

Wrinkles mean you laughed
Grey means you cared
Scars mean you lived

Arguing with fool only proves that there are two

Its words that encapsulate culture

I am not what you think I am but you are what you think I am

Being normal is not a virtue it denotes lack of courage

Others are not the answer for your happiness

Don't let anyone determine who you are

Come on, unleash your inner vulture

Grave yard tourism – making hue on suicides of common people by politicians

---

It's not the mountain that we conquer but ourselves

Pulling her out of buffet line for …..

You can't buy your way out of this criminal mistake

'Yo – Yo' diplomacy'

Wrapping themselves in layers of debts

The policy never works unless background conditions producing poverty are addressed

---

It's in democratic citizens nature to be like a leaf that doesn't believe in the tree its part of

---

The reactive modern cynic may dismiss this as vacant fodder of self help book

---

Outgrow the illusory ego shelf

The way to get things done is not to mind who get the credit for doing them
   - Benjamin Jowett

It would stultify rights provided under constitution

Let us trade our confessions

In his death he has become an ideological stick that can be brandished in any direction

---

Cosmic solitude

All you need is less

Unnecessary martyrs

Insurance add
'Buy before you cry'

The trouble with words is that you never know whose mouths they've been in

---

Three most harmful addictions –
Heroine, carbohydrates and monthly salary

Infectious pessimism

Success is no longer about changing strategies more often, but having the agility to execute multiple strategies concurrently

---

Whenever I have a problem I sing then I realize that my voice is far worse than my problem

---

War is cultural innovation, not intrinsic to human race

When life is sweet say thank you and celebrate; when life is bitter say thank you and grow

---

Driven by calculation; not compassion

World is waiting for markets to crash

Markets are waiting for your patience to crash

When you don't know what you are talking about, it is hard to know when you have finished

---

I searched for meaning of politics – poly means many; tics means blood suckers

---

When our memories outweigh our dreams, we have grown old

We always have death and taxes, but death does not get worse every year

---

It was while making newspaper deliveries, trying to miss the bushes and hit the Porch, that I first learned the importance of accuracy in journalism
   - CHARLES OSGOOD

Part of what makes human beings is imperfections

Words are things; and a small drop of ink

Falling like dew upon a thought produces

That which makes thousands, perhaps millions, think
   - Byron

It foreshadows our dystopian climate future

He is rich enough to avoid the worst of mess his habits have helped create

---

Pushing the limits of planet's ecology

Pregnancy, the most beautiful and essential task of human being…

Epidemiological apartheid

Fossil fuel habits

In the city smog is so bad that a mask is fashion accessory

It's so cold outside I saw a politician with hands in his own pocket!!!

Collusive nexus between corrupt politicians and big business men

---

If you kill a killer the number of killers on earth remains same

---

Instead of buying your kids all the things you never had, teach them all the things you were never taught

---

It takes nothing to stand in the crowd but takes everything to stand alone

---

Convergence of evidence

There are dark shadows on the earth, but its lights are stronger in the contrast.
   - Charles Dickens

Art meets smart
- Ad of smart phone company

Don't take your orgasm on my wall

Made of different flesh and blood

Day long breakfast!!!!

Let's put our optimism goggles on

Every country has to have Minister of Future

I wanted to hardwire competitiveness in Europe

For workers there are no jobs on a dead planet

Prayer is when you talk to God;
Meditation is when God talks to you

You are entirely bonkers
But I will tell you truth
All the best people are

Heart wrenching

The canker of corruption, blighting the upper echelons of system....

Even rags I am God
Fallen I am divine
High I stand when down trod
Long I live when slayed

Massive respect

Your "I can" is more important than your "IQ"

Some people are so poor, all they have is money

The best apology is change in behavior

Political parties are cocking a snook at real issues

The issue is politicians' leitmotif today

Beauty is not caused, it is

Two things are infinite, the Universe and the human stupidity and I am not sure about Universe

---

India's body shop industry is becoming hard to write off as a passing fad
- Forbes

Bitter or better. Either you take what has been dealt to you and allow it to make you better person or allow to tear you down. Choice belongs to you not fate

---

Fox, guarding the hen house

A one horse race

His patience is wearing thin

A dystopian feminist

I am more than the labels people stick on me

In our country not paying bribes is a competitive disadvantage

---

All those moments will be lost in time ….

Like tears in rain

I didn't just want to attend parties; I wanted the power to make them fail

---

My mind rebels at stagnation … give me problems, more problems

---

Hardest thing to learn in life is which bridge to cross and which bridge to burn

---

When Missionaries arrived the Afrikaans had land
And the Missionaries had the Bible
They taught us how to pray with our eyes closed
When we opened them they had the land and we have the Bible

Hungriest wolf in the pack

If we could quantify the totality of lost contributions and innovations as a result of prejudice, I believe we would find it staggering

---

Delhi always can't see beyond a meter blinded by fog, pollution and power

---

By the skin of your teeth

Ground the pavement

Shoot from the hip

Let the chips fall where they may

He doubles down his opinion in this state

He is capable of as many different positions on the issue as it is expedient to take

---

"4 am" knows all my secrets

When a woman's ring finger has the same size with the man's little finger they are meant to be

---

Not a shred of evidence exists in favor of the idea that life is serious

---

Here's some advice:

At a job interview, tell them you're willing to give 110 percent.

Unless the job is a statistician

If con is the opposite of pro, then isn't Congress the opposite of progress?

An endangered animal is eating an endangered plant and damaging an endangered planet

---

War is God's way of teaching us Geography

Never try to tell everything you know, it may take too short a time

---

Never trust a man when he is in love, drunk or running for office

---

When dignity requires privilege democracy has lost its way

Becoming huge part of life

Brutally honest

She has bettered even Lata Mangeshkar in rendition

Beautiful twist of expectations

Our leaders are conditioned to believe that any military involvement in a foreign land would necessarily turn into a quagmire

---

Capitalists' hyena press

Advertisement about yellow pages -
Let your fingers do the walking

Advertisement about inner wear
– What nature has forgotten we have fixed with cotton

Advertisement of Red Cross
– The greatest tragedy is indifference

Advertisement of Mac Pro
– Beauty outside, beast inside

Harley Davidson's advertisement.
-American by birth, rebel by choice

Bank's Advertisement
-Good people to grow with

Rise in lynch-mob hysteria

Writers like teeth are divided into incisors and grinders

It's important to bear in mind that political campaigns are designed by the same people who sell tooth paste and detergents

---

Statistically improbable "coin toss luck"

Harsh transition

Maintaining ego as President and integrating humility as well

---

At the center of the Universe dwells the Great Spirit and that center is there everywhere. It's in each one of us

---

The citizen will cross the oceans to fight for democracy but not cross street to vote for elections

---

Win or lose we go shopping after the elections

Every election is advance auction sale of stolen goods

Teaching is one profession that creates all other professions

---

India is the only country where people fight to be called "backward" and non - backward people curse for not being backward.

Let me never fall into the vulgar mistake of dreaming that I am persecuted whenever I am contradicted.

It's time to take back our God from those who have disgraced His message

---

The mark of the educated man is not in his boast that he has built his mountain of facts and stood on the top of it, but in his admission that there may be other peaks in the same range with men on the top of them, and that, though their views of the landscape may be different from his, they are nonetheless legitimate.
   - E.J. Pratt

We never notice the beauty because we are too busy trying to create it

---

Distance yourself from negative

Teachers don't teach for income, they teach for outcome

Attract what you expect
Reflect what you desire

Become what you respect
Mirror what you admire

Smile is a curve that makes anything straight

Staggering vanity of powerful people

Past is lesion not life sentence

Before you assume try this crazy method called asking

The war consigned the entire generation to the edge of civilization

---

I can't promise to fix all problems but I can promise you won't have to face them alone

---

Everyone cares when it's too late

It solidified my understanding that when all people have the power to share their experience the world will make progress

---

Life is too ironic.
It takes sadness to know what happiness is,
Noise to appreciate silence

Absence to value presence

You gave your lives without batting an eyelid in extreme pain

---

Leadership by title and by behavior is entirely different

Entire new layer of reality

Failure is sometimes out of way to reach intended route

No party has monopoly on wisdom

Inveterate liar who knows which side the bread is buttered

One who really loves you, loves you with dirt
  - An African saying

I trust you, but my trust and your bones will be broken at a time
  - Wife to her husband

To build a life that doesn't need a vacation from

To learn who rules over you simply find out who you are not allowed to criticize

---

The ebullient thread of people was like a river in spate

The surge of new leaders marks public outrage with the rigged system

---

Problems with communists, too left for liberals and too liberal for leftists

---

Only in love are unity and duality not in conflict

Reason makes possible the calculations, science and technological advances of industrial civilization, but reason does not connect us with forces of life

---

It shows perverse times we live in

Problems as stop lines and problems as guide lines

While they all fall in love with her smile, she waits for one who will fall in love with her scars

---

Biological and Career clock are in total conflict

A ham handed attempt to foil the protest

"Lexophile" is a term used to describe those who are clever with words, such as "you can tune a piano but you can't tuna fish" or "to write with a broken pencil is pointless."

A competition to see who can come up with the best lexphillies is held every year in Dubuque, Iowa. The year's winning submissions:

...A thief who stole a calendar got twelve months.

... The batteries were given out free of charge.

... A dentist and a manicurist married. They fought tooth and nail.

... A will is a dead giveaway.

... With her marriage, she got a new name and a dress.

... A boiled egg is hard to beat.

... Police were called to the daycare centre, where a three-year-old was resisting a rest.

.. Did you hear about the fellow whose whole left side was cut off? He's all right now.

... A bicycle can't stand alone; it is two tired.

... The guy who fell onto an upholstery machine is now fully recovered.

... He had a photographic memory which was never developed.

... When she saw her first strands of grey hair thought she'd dye.

... Acupuncture is a job well done. That's the point of it.

I chose a lazy person to do hard job because lazy person finds an easy way to do it
  - Bill Gates

His conduct eroded the gravity of serious discussion before us

---

Politics as a profession is systematic organization of hatred

---

The inner is the foundation of the outer
The still is the master of the restless

Crony capitalism

When you are dead you don't know that you are dead. It's difficult for others. Same is with your stupidity

---

You can't pour from an empty cup take care of yourself

In short, it is a struggle between those who would lay claim to India as a democratic, heterogeneous, inclusive and at least incipiently egalitarian national project, and those for whom nationalism has devolved into a lethal cocktail of aggressive religious assertion and equally ferocious unbridled capitalist growth, where neither the body count nor widening inequality indices matter

---

Weather wary Indian farmers resort to another cash crop – blood

---

The issue is pushed out of my mind horizon

Reading is dreaming with open eyes

If swimming is good for figure, explain whale to me

What a strange machine man is! You fill him with bread, wine, fish, and radishes, and out comes sighs, laughter, and dream

---

There was never a night or a problem that could defeat sunrise or hope.
- Bernard Williams

Pushed out of mind horizon

Deep down under the suppressing work of your heart, you know God exists
- An Atheist

Accept my past

Support my present

Encourage my future

See the people as they are not as we are

Swimming in ocean of information but sinking in ignorance

Reverse mind game

With activism being marked by astonishing sets of certitude, it was only natural that the institutional ambience would turn roguish once there was challenge to the existing ideological eco system

---

He was useful idiot in more sinister game of enemies

Flat footed police

Even Intellectual permissiveness has also its limits

Living for something beyond yourself

Brevity is the soul of wit
The two liners are proof

-The difference between in laws and outlaws

Outlaws are wanted

-Alcohol is perfect solvent it dissolves

Families, marriages and careers

-A fine is tax for doing wrong

A tax is fine for doing right

- Archaeologist: someone whose career lies in ruins

Archaeologist is the best husband any women can have

The older she gets, the more interested she becomes in her

-There are two kinds of people who do not say much

Those who are quiet and those who talk a lot

-They say that alcohol kills slowly

So what who is in hurry?

-Alcohol and calculus don't mix

Never drink and derive

-One nice thing about egoists

They don't talk about others

He is not stupid; he is smart knowing what stupid people want

---

1/4th of what you eat keeps you alive, 3/4th of what you eat keeps your doctor alive

---

Optimist invents aero plane and pessimist invents parachute

Putting historians in boondocks

The way we talk to our children becomes their inner voice

Money not only talks it also silences

97% of people who quit soon are employed by rest 3% who never gave up

---

Not all who wander are lost

A developed nation is not where poor use cars but rich use public transport

---

All of us must stand for free speech or lose it

Be happy without reason
You will be happy in every season

Do not take life too seriously. You will never get of it alive

---

Too much agreement kills chat

Wrong scale to measure nationalism

Politics is method of ruling divided people without undue violence

---

Everyone you meet is fighting a battle you knew nothing about

---

Politics is a mechanism to transfer wealth from those who work to those who vote

---

Disruptive technologies

Remote nationalism

Let the whisper count more than shout

Special pass to side step life challenges

Don't treat your self like an afterthought

If a guy wants you for your breasts, thighs or legs, send him to KFC. You are not a meal

---

Some times silence is more powerful than having the last word

---

Massive success is the best revenge

Trying to enhance the swimming abilities of ducks by throwing eggs in the water

---

Wait for good days is getting longer

If there be such a thing as truth it must infallibly be struck out by collision of mind with mind

---

Reining in lose canons of his own party

Sometimes you will never know true value of moment until it becomes a memory

---

Iterative manner

Break silo – intensify cross functional reaction

Number crunching

His mentality is infection and if turns out to be gangrene it warrants amputation

---

Inner child and inner idiot coming out intermittently

It is not our interest to pay principle and principle to pay interest
- A loan defaulter

Smiling has always been easier than explaining why I am sad

When you have a chronic illness you find out two things who really loves you and how strong you really are

---

The soldiers have paid their neglect in blood

It took less than an hour to make the atoms, a few hundred million years to make the stars and planets, but five billion years to make man

---

Patriarchal conservative thought process

Two most important days in your life, the day you are born and the day you have realized why you are born

---

If people treat you like an option, leave them like choice

This is not a game one can win, so lets respect both positions

---

10% of any population is cruel no matter what, 10% of is merciful, no matter what, 80% could be moved in either direction

---

The path obscured by confusion
The walk continued by courage

A high pitched drama but with jerky narration

Fitgtive pension world

Freedom from fear of failing has made us to win

Everything is pre-written but with prayers it can be re-written

---

Competitive screeching in the Parliament

Failing interestingly

Its in the democratic citizens nature to be like a leaf that doesn't believe in the tree its part of

---

Things turn out best for the people who make the best of the way things turn out

---

State doesn't bestow rights and agreement with state actors can not be conditionality for rights

---

The Paper has stood up in defense of democracy and upholding the right of citizen to democratic dissent. Let not the religious groups knee jerk that media and civil society speak out only against their brand of intolerance and fascism

---

The Calculus of Consent has long ago debunked the decisions of the majority state as "sacrosanct". Parliamentary system of governance does not imply the "dominance" of the rulers. State is a cooperative venture among individuals and the state must reflect their interests and concerns

---

Even as some have reason to think "the incidents" … are public goods, others could have reason to think that they are public bad. Those who think that something is a "bad" have as much right to inform contestational public opinion and action - as those who influence acquiescence.

Open your eye

&

Close your I

Contrarian debates are valuable particularly when an action/decision/law could have huge externalities on

330

everyday lives, democracy, freedom of ideas and their expression/ communication

---

The story of a self made man

General water to Mineral water!!!!

Everyone knows that liabilities and externalities are most borne by the weakest and the benefits garnered by the most powerful. The state then cannot be the sovereign interlocutor and defender of the people

---

One only wishes that the state shows the same MACHO in caring for and protecting the weak, in getting back fugitives from law and black money and national wealth spirited out and in valuing each of its citizens as its MACHO in driving a wedge between "agitators" and the nation.

There can be no anticipatory restraint on free speech

There is no justice without access to justice.

While arguing a case in the Supreme Court recently, I had occasion to tell the judges, "Your tragedy is you enter a court from the back door, you don't see what is written over your heads. I enter from the front door, the first thing I see every morning is Satyameva Jayate."

When they call attendance senators do not know whether to say present or not guilty

---

When people wave at me they are using all fingers. The esteem of nation really has gone up

Carter

Recession is when your neighbor loses his job

Depression is when you lose yous

Recovery is when Jimmy Carter loses his

His incisive spell is an elixir that is needed in this time of distress

From **Regina Brett, interesting one liners**

- When you don't get what you want, you get something better—experience.
- Everything changes when you change.
- Burying your talents won't make them grow.
- What they call you is up to them. What you answer to is up to you.
- In this drama of life, there are no small parts.
- Give others a second chance to make a first impression.
- Every job is as magical as you make it.
- There's a time for everything but not always at the same time.
- If you're going to doubt anything, doubt your doubts.
- Sometimes the job you want is the job you already have.
- Most of the time, the only person in your way is you.
- Sometimes your mission is revealed moment by moment.
- When things fall apart, they could actually be falling into place.

- When you fail, fail forward.
- Choice, not just chance, determines your destiny.
- It's not about what you can do, but what God can do through you.
- Instead of trying to be the best in the world, be the best for the world.
- It's important to know both your superpower and your kryptonite.
- Not everything that counts can be counted.
- Don't confuse your work with your worth.
- Clear the path for the person who comes after you.
- Just because someone isn't on your path doesn't mean they're lost.
- Expand your comfort zone to make others more comfortable.
- There's no whining on the yacht.
- No one can drain you without your permission.
- The world needs people who are fully alive.
- To find out who you are, let go of who you aren't.
- Align yourself first, then take action.
- The most important boss to answer to is the small, still voice within.
- Power is an inside job.
- It's up to you to launch your life.
- Things don't happen to you, they happen for you and for others.
- Don't die with your music in you.
- Nothing you want is upstream, so stop struggling.

- Create a pocket of greatness right where you are.
- Even when you feel invisible, your work isn't.
- You make a living by what you get; you make a life by what you give.
- Be somebody's hero.
- For networking to work, we all have to be the net.
- If you don't want regrets at the end of your life, have no regrets at the end of each day.
- Find your grail. Be who God meant you to be, and you will set the world on fire.
- Get busy on the possible.
- Start where you are.
- You can make a big difference no matter how little you make.
- Magnify the good.
- Do your best and forget the rest. Pay no attention to the results. It could simply be too soon to tell.
- We all do the same things. It's how we do them.
- Interruptions are divine assignments.
- Adjust your own oxygen mask before helping others or you'll be of no use to anyone – including you.
- Instead of treating people the way you want to be treated, treat people the way they want to be treated.
- If you want to see a miracle, be the miracle.
- Everyone matters to somebody.

- Speak up for others, especially when they aren't present to speak up for themselves.
- Give birth to yourself every day.
- Sometimes it's enough to make one person happy.
- The secret of life is no secret. It's sprinkled all over your life.
- If you can't be the rock, be the ripple.
- Give as if the world is your family, because it is.
- Everyone is either your student or your teacher. Most people are both.
- Pray like you mean it.
- Arrive early.
- Dream big.
- Consult your own soul. Deep inside you already know the answers you need.
- Get in the game.
- God doesn't always call the strong. Sometimes you have to be weak enough to serve.
- When you have nothing but faith, you have enough.
- Be a good monk. Make your life a prayer.
- Believe in abundance.
- Shine your light, no matter how dark the world around you appears
- Comfort the sick. When everyone else flees, be the one who stays.
- You have an endless supply of abundance from a wealthy Father who loves you, and so does everyone else.
- Carry as you climb.

- Be an original. Forge your own path.
- Harness the power of hope.
- Watch well your words. Practice restraint of tongue and pen.
- The world needs your Yes!
- Use your power.
- You are a child's most important teacher.
- What you think about you bring about.
- Aim higher.
- Make someone else's dream come true.
- Triage.
- A saint is someone who knows how much God loves them.
- Don't quit before the miracle happens.
- Make amends as soon as you can, while you still can.
- Silence the noise. In times of doubt or indecision, pause and make room for God.
- To be a channel of peace, you have to stay open.
- God will not have His work made manifest by cowards.
- Leave a legacy time can't erase.
- If you woke up today, God isn't through with you yet.
- Life isn't fair, but it's still good.
- When in doubt, just take the next small step.
- Life is too short to waste time hating anyone.
- Don't take yourself so seriously. No one else does.
- Pay off your credit cards every month.

- You don't have to win every argument. Agree to disagree.
- Cry with someone. It's more healing than crying alone.
- It's OK to get angry with God. He can take it.
- Save for retirement starting with your first paycheck.
- When it comes to chocolate, resistance is futile.
- Make peace with your past so it won't screw up the present.
- It's OK to let your children see you cry.
- Don't compare your life to others'. You have no idea what their journey is all about.
- If a relationship has to be a secret, you shouldn't be in it.
- Everything can change in the blink of an eye. But don't worry; God never blinks.
- Life is too short for long pity parties. Get busy living, or get busy dying.
- You can get through anything if you stay put in today.
- A writer writes. If you want to be a writer, write.
- It's never too late to have a happy childhood. But the second one is up to you and no one else.
- When it comes to going after what you love in life, don't take no for an answer.
- Burn the candles, use the nice sheets, wear the fancy lingerie. Don't save it for a special occasion. Today is special.
- Over prepare, then go with the flow.

- Be eccentric now. Don't wait for old age to wear purple.
- The most important sex organ is the brain.
- No one is in charge of your happiness except you.
- Frame every so-called disaster with these words: "In five years, will this matter?"
- Always choose life.
- Forgive everyone everything.
- What other people think of you is none of your business.
- Time heals almost everything. Give time time.
- However good or bad a situation is, it will change.
- Your job won't take care of you when you are sick. Your friends will. Stay in touch.
- Believe in miracles.
- God loves you because of who God is, not because of anything you did or didn't do.
- Whatever doesn't kill you really does make you stronger.
- Growing old beats the alternative - dying young.
- Your children get only one childhood. Make it memorable.
- Read the Psalms. They cover every human emotion.
- Get outside every day. Miracles are waiting everywhere.
- If we all threw our problems in a pile and saw everyone else's, we'd grab ours back.

- Don't audit life. Show up and make the most of it now.
- Get rid of anything that isn't useful, beautiful or joyful.
- All that truly matters in the end is that you loved.
- Envy is a waste of time. You already have all you need.
- The best is yet to come.
- No matter how you feel, get up, dress up and show up.
- Take a deep breath. It calms the mind.
- If you don't ask, you don't get.
- Yield.
- Life isn't tied with a bow, but it's still a gift..

Historic upset

Maturing is realizing that how many things don't require your comments

---

Unguarded thoughts

Pensive thinker

Obsessive fan

When people react with anger or hostility to your boundaries you have found the edge where their respect for you ends

---

Job is not what I am getting it's what I am becoming

Return of paternalism

With more repression comes greater expression

Between what is said and not meant and what is meant and not said, lots of love is lost

---

With this policy the Govt has ended up with egg on its face

Breaching the incompatibility wall

Granite face

Attitude is contagious make yours worth catching

What consumes your mind controls your life

Meditation is not controlling thought it's to stop letting them control you

---

During the day I don't believe ghosts. During night I am little open minded !!!

Never say a thing that could not stand as the last thing you have ever said

---

Never let the things you want make you forget the things you have

---

Thanks from bottom of my heart

This in an era that doesn't aggrandize leaders and presidents, but shrinks them.

"Man is puny in the face of destiny."

Many presidents fared better in history than in office. But it would be a morale booster and a sign of civic maturity if more Americans appreciated what an exceptional president they have right now. It could be a long wait for the next one.

This is, of course, perverse liberal-media propaganda

It's wobbly centrism to a left-flank frustrated

If changing minds with a keypad is a fool's errand; I'm surely a fool, but not on that count. I simply offer some points for the open-minded to ponder

---

A gutsy political risk

---

constant, kabuki-style congressional votes to repeal.

An epic triumph

Properly canonizing the black

Pseudo-scandals

Carnal antics

He has weathered a recession, invisible racism, a reckless Republican Congress, a lily-livered Democratic Party,

---

Press corps under existential pressure to deliver page views and Nielsen ratings

---

Obama isn't a performer like Reagan or a preacher like Clinton. He's head over heart, cool over warm. Yet he did his pastoral duties

---

It is harder than ever to see the big canvas and thus find fresh perspectives. We view current events as puny rivers of Tweets, not grand chapters in the ultimate story – history

---

Slaves by chains and by debts

Shining like Sun needs burning like Sun

They tried to bury us, but they don't know we are seeds

Deeply perceptive and even deeply prophetic essay

There are no traffic jams on the extra mile

India's moon shot

Its second class street for me

The idea is not square with the truth

Things that you have packed in your heart beneath waters of consciousness

---

Do you have anything to declare?
Yes I declare this is stupidity

You never know how strong you are until being strong is the only choice ---

Rewire your brain to be happy

Mistakes are proof of trials

I am full of sparkles and compassion

If size mattered, elephant should be the king of jungle

He is made of straw;

Dwell in their energy; see only essence of the person not shell

---

You will lust after the beauty and infatuated by it

Connect to inner self of the person, then physical imperfections disappear and become irrelevant

---

You have to love yourself enough so that any other love just adds candles to cake, you have already iced

---

His epic take down of opposition over the issue

Left Right binaries needs to be replaced with what works

I can give best to others if I am in touch with the best in myself

---

Growth for the sake of growth is the ideology of cancer cells

---

Gold medals are not really made of gold, they are made of SWEAT, DITERMINATION ... and hard to find alloy called GUTS

If today were the last day of your life would you want to do what you are about to do today?

May be if we tell people brain is an app, then they start using it

---

When words make noise silence can talk

Daughterly guilt

I never lose either I win or I learn

Being a woman is terribly difficult trade since it consists principally of dealing with men

---

Let no one ever come to you without leaving happier
Mother Teresa

Far too much law for those who can afford and far
little for those who cannot afford

Humor is the most engaging cowardice

Protesting against society's refusal to protect dignity of
individual itself confers dignity on the individual

Don't limit child to your learning for he was born in
another time

Vote him, everyone else will send your children to war
A caption in Presidential elections

Conformity may give you a quiet life; it may even
bring you to a University Chair. But all change in
history, all advance, comes from the nonconformists.
If there had been no trouble-makers, no dissenters, we
should still be living in caves.

   -A.J.P. Taylor

You are not in the universe, you are universe
An intrinsic part of it

Ultimately you are not a person

But a focal point where the universe is becoming conscious of itself

What an amazing miracle

Spending money they haven't earned

Buying things they don't want

Impress people they don't like

Festival can survive without H2O

But the country can't

Nationalism does nothing but teach you to hate people you never met

And to take pride in accomplishments you had not part in

Introverts unite separately in your own home

Thinking is difficult that's why most people judge

Farmers grow crops online

People have to down load and eat !!!

The reader ceases to be reader and instead becomes writer

The Mantra of online writing

We never know the worth of water till the well is dry

Leave the people better than you found them

Perpetual idiosyncrasy of educated

Abdication of educated from responsibilities

Since the ancient discipline with roots in Hinduism and Buddhism became a popular exercise in the west, yogis have inundated popular culture with their pursuit of that elusive calm in a rapidly spinning world

---

To take fresh hair cut to turn profits

Drink deeply
Ad of coffee

He took significant bite of opposition lead

We had future until you started destroying it

Tomorrow is one day closer to another wrinkle
Ad of old age pension scheme

Pixilated

Laughter is the closest distance between two persons

Our fundamental test consists of our attitude towards those who are at our mercy: Animals.
And in this respect we have suffered a debacle so fundamental that all others stem from it

---

Perfection is limit less accumulation of imperfections

When you step into corporate life make sure you have right stepped

---

The distance between insane and genius is success

The giant in front of you is never bigger than the God in side you

---

There are many complications behind the incident which are hard to understand

---

If I had 9 hours to chop a tree I will spend first 6 sharpening my ax

---

All differences in this world are of degree and not of kind because oneness is the secret of everything
Swamy Vivekananda

Be selective about your battles sometimes peace is better than being right

---

He is secretly putting me down

When you start finding your worth you will find it harder to stay around people who don't

---

If you are not dead yet your are not done yet

Carbon negative country

Carbon neutral country

Carbon sink country

"His terrorist is not my terrorist approach"

Work like someone is working 24 hours a day to take it away from you

---

Comparison is thief of joy

Unshakable conviction

Be reflection of what you would like to receive

About the Author

 Dr. R. Divakar is PhD in Rural Development with specialization in "Institutional Development at Grassroots for Poverty Alleviation": He has done M.Sc., (Ag) in Agricultural Sciences.

He has served Syndicate Bank, a Public Sector Bank in India across the country. He worked for UNDP on a SAARC project of Poverty Alleviation. In addition he served CARE India, Naandi Foundation and Swayam Krishi Sangam, in Senior Positions, all reputed for their work in Professional Development field. He consults World Vision International for Mongolia, India and Asia Pacific Regions. He has played lead role in the implementation of CGAP and Ford Foundation sponsored global initiative "Graduation Approach" to eradicate extreme poverty. It's implemented in 3 continents and many of the practices are standardized by Dr. Divakar are in vogue. He consults Concern World Wide, an Irish non-profit for its Afghanistan operations. Dr. Divakar is also associated with Sydney University Business School for its mission of "doing business with the poor". At present Dr. Divakar is Program Lead for ACCESS Development Services, a non-profit working in India on agriculture front.

Dr. Divakar is also a passionate farmer and prolific writer. His 33 year journey in Development field has resulted in collection of excellent English words and phrases which he has painstakingly compiled to shape this book.

In his long journey in the field of Professional Development and Poverty Practices, he has passionately collected good words and usages to pass it on to next generation of netizen.

"Let your train of thought not derail for there will be no survivors"

Printed in the United States
By Bookmasters